What readers are saying about
Ordinary People as Monks and Mystics . . .

"The book is terrific. It has given me—and I am sure many others—a lot to think about on what is really the one subject of ultimate importance—our place in creation and our relation to the Creator. . . . a wonderful blend of the modern and the traditional."

"So much of what it says connects for me, as I'm in the position of being an extrovert who needs the social contact yet also needs the contemplative dimension in daily life."

"I am savoring it—read a few pages a day. *Ordinary People as Monks and Mystics* is a great help in understanding myself, and I feel more content in being 'my self'."

"Thanks for a *whole* book of positive thinking. . . . Here are unsung heroes, monks and mystics who have much to share, a light to shine, and wisdom to spare . . . "

" . . . I'm sure this will not be the last time I turn to it. It's the kind of book that is both reassuring and challenging. Reassuring in that I agree with its description of 'wholeness' . . . challenging in that it gives the subject a completely new dimension. It defines an entirely new set of goals which I hope to move toward, however, slowly."

"I enjoyed reading *Ordinary People as Monks and Mystics*. I found it to be very uplifting."

"The book and the questionnaire fascinated me."

"The title attracted me immediately and I was deeply engrossed in it from page one. . . . I am a very ordinary person living a very ordinary life and I appreciate the faith this book has in the ordinary. I also appreciate the encouragement it offers people in their ability to actualize themselves and the way it has removed the pressure of time from such a journey. . . . "

" . . . an intimate forum of religious and spiritual thought."

" . . . extraordinary!"

"The book makes a great deal of sense to me from the inside out."

"This philosophical tour de force is enjoyable!—Though not speed reading!"

"I have passed along *Ordinary People as Monks and Mystics* to others as well as recommended it to many. I am hoping to have an opportunity to use the book in a class—or at least have it available for recommended reading."

"Marsha Sinetar is a marvelous teacher."

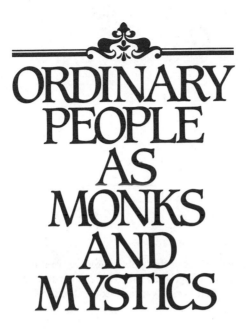

ORDINARY PEOPLE AS MONKS AND MYSTICS

Lifestyles for Self-discovery

Marsha Sinetar

PAULIST PRESS
New York/Mahwah

Library of Congress
Catalog Card Number: 85-62932

ISBN: 0-8091-2773-3

Published by Paulist Press
997 Macarthur Boulevard
Mahwah, New Jersey 07430

Printed and bound in the
United States of America

Contents

Dear Friend,

I saw your ad . . . and probably qualify for your project.

After moving south with my wife and stepchildren in 1980, I'm now a hermit in the woods. My wife died close to two years ago, and her sons subsequently moved out.

I'm 52, run a [small business] by myself and go 'out' three times a week. There are no utilities here. I pump water, cut wood and take batteries out for recharging. I enjoy the solitude and try (not always effectively) to conduct my business as a service. I'm also committed to preserving my land as wilderness.

Sincerely, Boxholder, Alabama.

Acknowledgements

It has been said that whoever finds out what is, for him, good, and holds fast to it, will become whole. This is such a simple truth, yet so difficult for most of us to carry out in life.

The people in this small, uncomplicated study are fine teachers about just this work: Each puts his own words and special mark upon the task of becoming whole. Yet, as a group, those in this book speak in a single voice about the costs and values of actualization—which is but another name for wholeness. By their life-examples and statements they show what actualization requires of us.

I've tried to quote each person as accurately as possible. Given the fact that, in writing a book, style and clarity must also be taken into account, in some cases I've edited their comments. To the best of my knowledge, their sentiments and intent have been kept intact.

Personally, I must acknowledge two persons who helped with the initial reading and editing of this material. To my neighbor, and most talented friend, Patricia Ditzler, who read and edited the earliest chapters of this book, and who so encouraged me along the way, I owe a tremendous debt of gratitude. To my project editor and most patient colleague, Dianna Molvig, who manicured and organized each chapter, I say thank you. There is no way that someone with a work, writing and travel schedule like mine could have remained faithful to the requirements and enormous task of writing a book without the ongoing encouragement, optimism and support of such fine colleagues.

I would also like to say how much I enjoyed working with Georgia J. Mandakas my editor at Paulist Press who made the process of putting the book together both effective and smooth. I did not expect a long-distance editorial relationship to become a fast friendship. The whole experience turned out to be a happy surprise.

To each study participant, I must also express my deepest thanks. For joining the study in the first place, for having had the trust and openness to answer my questions when I was but a stranger, for inviting me into their homes, for giving me such generous amounts of telephone time for follow-up conversations, for having had the faith that something positive and productive would come of our interviews, for writing me letters packed with self-disclosures of the most personal kind, for sending me their favorite scriptural and literary quotations and experiential wisdom—I am enormously touched and appreciative. All the participants' willingness to be truthful, their natural eagerness to confront and—where possible—resolve the deepest issues of life, their simple dignity in conveying the values, organizing priorities and needs of their life, have made this study a joy for me.

Introduction

My bias is this: ordinary, everyday people can and do become whole. They can and do live in ways that express their highest and most cherished values—values which also happen to be those most prized universally and collectively throughout human history. People who become whole are the ones who find completeness by consciously integrating inner and outer realities. This is a book about such persons, and about the way in which they manage to merge their inner truths with the demands of everyday living. It is for them, and for all who long for their own wholeness, that this book is written and dedicated.

Ordinary people can and do inspire others into healthier, more mature choices and behaviors. They can live as good stewards in their communities while simultaneously protecting their unique way of being in the world—a way of being which may be so idiosyncratic as to contradict and confound the logical expectations and mind-sets of those they would serve.

Ordinary people can and do resolve these and other contradictions alone, without guidance from experts or advice from friends and family. They themselves are our best experts and teachers of what it means to be self-sufficient and what it means to lead virtuous, courageous lives. This is a book about such persons, and it is for them—and for all who identify with them, who would be whole—that this book is written and dedicated.

My research began several years ago when my own inclination and interest made me pull away from the way I saw most people living, in favor of a more solitary, silent, reflective way of life. Although it isn't my purpose to describe my own life-experience in this book, every book is in some sense autobiographical, and surely this one is no exception. In a very real way, I am one of the subjects I studied.

This is a book about self-actualizing *and* self-actualized people. My research was driven by my own intuition of what it means to be and become self-actualized, as well as by my intense interest in the values of actualization and in the process itself. My day-to-day work is that of an organizational psychologist, mediator, and educator who for several years has been increasingly interested in the adult choices, life-styles and personalities of fully human, actualizing people. Both in my practice, where my clients often are purposeful, wholesome and actualizing, and in this research project where the values of actualization have been more sharply focused for me, I have felt that the healthiest personalities have much to teach about what it means to be mature, generous, virtuous, and even happy.

Self-actualization—that state of psychological wholeness or completeness, personality health and authenticity which first emerged as psychology, and as an idea, out of the inspirational work of Abraham Maslow—is now a phrase surrounded by much myth and commercialism. Some people believe that people cannot *be* actualized; that people are always in the process of becoming. That may or may not be true. Most self-help books, and even many psychological textbooks (directed at health care professionals), treat the topic as if only a rare person had self-actualizing tendencies. I see the matter differently. In later chapters, I will discuss how actualization is our species' most natural state.

But being actualized (and this is where I think the misunderstanding of the term has its roots) is not an *end point*. It is not a final or static destination at which a human being arrives, only to stop growing. It is a starting point, to my way of thinking, a birth—as may have been meant in the biblical phrase "born again"—of the converted personality, the personality which comes into its own wholeness of being. This conversion is so profound that after it life expresses itself through the personality in a completely revitalized and original manner—a manner which may even be hard to understand. I should add that my observations show me that most people are self-actualizing, not actualized, and that—like Maslow—for the purposes of simplicity and ease of expression, most of the time I will refer to people as actualizing, not actualized. However, I also want to say that contrary to some, my hunch is that there are many more self-actualizing individuals around than we expect, and that more actualized people exist than we think and that these are quite natural manifestations of healthy human development.

I also believe that numbers grow yearly and that this increase has socio-economic ramifications as well. This is a subject I've written about in terms of its impact on American management[1] and need not elaborate here. But I should mention that some completely ordinary self-challenges are likely to be misinterpreted as problems (e.g., the "mid-life crisis" which many health care professionals, and certainly the media, have interpreted as a foolhardy, perhaps unnecessary, stage of life) by those who don't clearly recognize the issues of actualization when they see them.

It has been said that the inception of real personality health occurs when an individual stops trying to get the world to meet his needs and wants, and begins seeking out ways to perform some needed and meaningful service for others. That seems like a good and practical starting point for the discussion at hand, since it allows us to view wholeness through an inner/outer filter of how people conduct their life in relationship to others. This is helpful for several reasons. First, actualization involves some measure of pulling back, away from others. By viewing the process of growth as having within it one stage in which people move away from at least some part of social custom, we can better understand what is happening in our own lives when we make such moves. Later in the same process, the actualizing individual begins to relate to the external world through a fresh and truly generous perspective, and ultimately feels quite connected to others. Eventually the person begins to exhibit a level of caring for others that can be called service or stewardship.

Stewardship, as we shall see in a later chapter, is always unique in the actualizing person, and may not conform to what society or family may expect from the individual. For one person, environmental concerns may become hugely important in life. For another, especially the mystic type, art or poetry may be the gift that is given to others. In all cases, there are, as one research subject said, "a wonderful set of emotions" received from giving to others, caring for others, so much so that in the psychologically whole person social action is probably at its best. Throughout this book, I give concrete examples of how progressively healthy people are able to integrate their own needs, talents and values with the needs of others, the environment, the larger community. In doing this they serve self-and-other in highly creative, useful and fulfilling ways.

This book is also about two primary values of self-actualization, which I call "social transcendence" and "self-transcendence." These are characteristics which the actualizing personality has in one degree or another. Probably, although I'm not sure and have made little attempt to measure, the greater degree of each, the greater the degree of actualization. Neither of these terms is original; each has been explored as routes to human liberation in the great literature, religion, art and philosophy of mankind. Perhaps this was what Jesus of

Nazareth was talking about when he said, "He who finds his life will lose it, and he who loses his life for my sake will find it" (Mt 10:39), since both social and self transcendence involve a letting go of the old secure ways, a dying to the old self, and a move into unknown, unchartered territories of the self.

A cursory definition of social and self-transcendence may help at this point to put these terms more clearly into our understanding. By *social transcendence* I mean emotional independence or detachment from societal influences, even from other people when necessary. I call the monk one who had detached emotionally from a known, familiar and comfortable way of life in order to embark on an uncharted inner journey. The monk responds to an inner call, reinterprets his basic way of being in the world—which might include reinterpreting the way he relates to others, work, marriage, Church or other organizational status, and even includes a renewed definition of himself and his basic place in the scheme of things.

And I mean more: I use the term monk without reference to gender, material status, occupation, or place of residence, and with full knowledge that people I'd call monks would not and do not, in fact, call themselves monks.

I simply needed a term which would embrace the person who, due to an inner prompting, turns from familiar, secure patterns of social custom, relationship and community life toward something altogether unknown. I needed a word which embraced the imagery of silence, dignity and obedience which automatically accompanies a person when he embarks upon an interior journey, whatever route that may take and whatever the cost.

By *self-transcendence* I mean having experienced, or experiencing in daily awareness, the mystical sense as it is classically described in poetry or religious literature. Maslow, for example, defined the peak experience as an "ecstatic moment" and as a "moment of rapture." He and others liken the experience to that of love. During these moments the self, the ego (one's separateness) disappears, melts, as the individual fuses experientially with the object(s) of perception: the cosmos or nature, his work—especially when he is producing an object or working on a craft—sometimes even with another, as with a mother and child, although this is not the likeliest mystic fusion.

The great religious figures and saints were mystics in the way I use this word in this book. The great artists and poets are, as well, and they communicate their experiences to others through their work. I have simply searched for, and have found, a few ordinary people (i.e., non-saints, although one never can know, not great figures, in the way commonly meant) who nevertheless—like Dante, Blake, Whitman, Emerson, the Transcendentalists, Swedenborg, Holmes, Tennyson, St. Teresa, St. Paul, and others—have perceived themselves to be a part of the whole and have experienced a radical transformation or mysterious union with another reality or with God. I did not seek out, nor did I encourage interviews with, those whose main interest was what Evelyn Underhill calls magic: the occult, astrology, or other supernatural powers and psychic phenomena. My interest was and is purely that elevated moral sense, intuitional mind and unitive consciousness described in the great scriptural, literary and poetic works of mankind.

Only some of those I interviewed in this study are mystics, while several have had a mystical/peak experience and even are sensitive to the transformative power of that moment. I should also mention at this point that while there is, in human terms, no neat split between people who are monks (i.e., socially transcendent) and those who are mystics (self-transcendent), I have divided this book into two parts which treat each type as if it were distinct from the other. Of course, mystics may live as if they were monks, and monks can experience self-transcendence. It is also possible for monks (even those in a monasterial setting) to be highly legalistic, "organization men"—rational types who don't remember having had a transcendent experience, or who have no sympathy for the occurrence.

Of those I interviewed, enough spoke freely of their mystic sense and state of mind that I was moved to include their experiences and way of perceiving things in this book. Unlike those I call monks who wouldn't call themselves that, the mystic always knows that he or she is a mystic. Mystics are the ones who hunger and thirst after righteousness, as the Bible puts it, the ones who yearn for continued or increased union with the other reality they themselves feel is the *real* reality—the reality which heals and makes all things new again. Their yearning is their most distinctive mark and has been called by some a "deep and burning wound," because it propels them toward the transcendent nature of life much as a lover is drawn toward the object of his love. The term is also descriptive of the slow and painful completion process of joining totally with, or being in, the transcendent state—a process which should not be confused with psychological development. The latter is a matter of self-understanding, self-acceptance and personal integration. The former involves itself with self-forgetting, the disappearance of the self into mysterious union with God, the Absolute, the Transcendent aspect of reality, the Tao. Thus the term self-transcendence (with its emphasis on the small "s" in the word self, as opposed to the Self, higher aspect of the personality) means letting go of egoistic interests and practical, worldly matters.

I should also say something about the study itself and about how I located the participants. There was nothing sophisticated about my methodology; quite the contrary—I call it communication, pure and simple. I was willing to talk to any people (through a written survey first and later—if the survey response proved interesting to me and if the others were willing—through a personal interview, either face-to-face or by teleconference if they lived very far away) who felt they fit the characteristics listed in my ad.

My only screening device was their initial letter to me. Only three of the more than forty people who contacted me about the ad didn't fit my idea of the person I was looking for. Two of these three contacted me with postcards that were so illegible that I felt they'd have a lot of trouble with the lengthy survey form. The third sent a five-page, emotion-packed and quite disorganized letter which rambled on about pets and the occult.

I wanted to communicate with people who had pulled away *physically* as well as *perceptually* from conventional life. Although I come across many actualizing persons in the course of my professional practice, my feeling was that there is another, less traveled path in this process and so hoped to find people who could vividly represent social/self-transcendence for readers. I wanted to communicate with adults who have had to be responsible for the consequences for their choices (thus the age specification on the ad). And I hoped to locate self-actualizers, so I just listed several key qualities which actualizers possess, thinking that only someone with those qualities would respond favorably to the list.

My singlemost interest throughout the project was simply to communicate with individuals (a) who had pulled away, entered into what Thomas Merton calls "the wilderness" of their own interior journey, (b) yet who managed to stay connected to others through their work or community/social activities, in some positive, contributory way, and (c) who were drawn to the call of my ad for whatever reason. I felt it important to this discussion that each person in the study have a positive connection with society. This was essential to me for two main reasons: I wanted to concentrate my focus on those who were *functioning* in their communities in a contributive, effective manner, even though they might be undergoing many personal changes. My thought was that the solutions of such functioning would be very helpful to others who might be undergoing personal change, who might want to pull away, radically alter their lives, yet who needed, or desired, to stay connected in some viable way. I also am aware of one of the dangers of merely "pulling away," withdrawing, and that is the tendency to get too inward, passive, self-absorbed. At best, such tendencies are the high points of contemplation, the "let-it-be" attitude of non-doing which we read about in mystic and especially in Zen literature. At worst, pulling away can be a sign of an inability to function—at any time. It can signify a variety of personality problems, dullness, ineptitude or hostilities. I recall, for example, when I started the study that some friends who heard of my search for study participants told me of a man who lived as a hermit in the backwoods of northern California. "He's a poet," they said, and went on to describe the way in which he lived: barricaded in his small cabin with plenty of guns and ammunition to keep visitors and strangers away. That was not the kind of person I was looking for.

I hoped (through a simple communication process with actualizing people who were constructively active in the world) to learn something about their world-view, their way of solving problems and creating meaning in life. My sense was that if they had the rich inner life I hoped they would have, they would have something of value and elegance to teach others.

This book is organized into three parts. The first part focuses on the monk: his characteristics and some, but certainly not all, variations of life-style that might be fitting solutions for the socially transcendent person. The first part also presents patterns of similarity exhibited by the socially transcendent and provides interview comments to better illustrate the points being made. The second part deals with a definition, discussion and overview of the mystic state, and includes selected interview material to describe the characteristics presented. The third part is an exploration into the ways in which both social and self-transcendence are of value to personality health and how both elements help promote the actualization process itself.

Finally, I have no idea whether this material will add light to the field of spiritual psychology—the study of, to use Abraham Maslow's phrase, "the farther reaches" of the human spirit. This field is already brilliantly illumined by the writings of people such as R.M. Bucke, Evelyn Underhill, Abraham Maslow, and of course Thomas Merton, whose writings span theology, psychology, philosophy and poetry, and who has so deeply influenced my own life and work. I do know that the prompting to write about this subject and to do the research itself comes from directly within me. And so I have answered the call, however elementary the result.

Part One:

The Way of The Monk

1

Advancement to Wholeness

I have minimal possessions, no real ownership of anything much. No TV, for example. I read, and think, and
when I want to, I talk to friends. I'm self-entertaining,
for the most part. I'm living in a communal setting,
where everyone shares chores and works with one another. I've dropped out of a professional career and
now am working as a carpenter. [Carpenter, California]

In response to my asking what she thought constituted wholeness, a youthful client once answered, "It's making *aliyah*—
which is a Jewish term meaning ascension. To me, people are
whole when they have the guts to live out their convictions in their
lives, when they can face difficult situations and everyday choices
in a way that honors what's inside them." Her spontaneous remarks came far closer to hitting the mark than I had expected.

Wholeness exists to the extent an individual is conscious
of and receptive to his innermost self. The more aware and accepting a person becomes of his inner images and motivations,
the more he becomes healed. The Jungian analyst Gerhard Ad-
ler once wrote that the words "whole," "holy," and "heal" all
contain within them a deep and constant similarity—that they
all convey the idea that wholeness and healing are related. With
each of these elements, the personality becomes enriched and
gains the sort of personal power that blesses them. Moreover,
the true purpose and meaning of each life *is* wholeness—that

process my client called making *aliyah*. The advancement to wholeness is the real occupation of human existence.

As did my young client, when we think about our own growth we probably think simultaneously of two co-existing and equally necessary elements: self-knowledge (i.e., knowing who the self within us really is and awakening to the values, needs and wants of that self) *and* the ability—perhaps I should say the will—to act out that real self in our lives.

This close tie between knowing and doing can explain why, for many, self-knowledge is generally resisted. Certainly, it takes great courage to know ourselves as we truly are since this knowledge makes demands on us—demands not everyone wants to fulfill. For some, self-knowledge means letting go of the idealized image their intellect (and perhaps family or friends) thinks they "should" be. For these people, living out the real self may mean living quite unspectacular lives. For others, knowing the truth of their being may mean stretching into untried, frighteningly difficult arenas. Whatever the demand, when we know a thing to be true, then appropriate, responsive actions follow naturally and reflexly.

The subsequent choices are often painful, requiring that we alter our self-view and way of life, or let go of favored habits, perhaps even favored relationships. But choices such as these can be made quite creatively and boldly when we know what is to be done. Knowing ourselves is not by any means automatic, except, I should add, for the rare individual. For almost everyone, in order to accomplish the knowing part of the wholeness equation, courage and the will to know must be paired traits within the personality.

A fearful individual is a person held in check, stunted, even crippled—although his body may be perfectly formed. The longer fear persists, the more he is stuck and frozen, passively unable to express what he needs and knows he wants. In my practice, this type of fear can mask itself as anxiety, or as a disorderly, confused mind, incapable of thinking things through and incapable of identifying life-important answers. It can also mask itself as pseudo-stupidity, apathy, as a niceness which is irritating to self-and-other through its artificial appeasing quality. Even poor judgment can be a symptom of not-knowing: the effectiveness and potency of the person being buried under his miscalculating mind-set.

Paul Tillich's phrase, "the courage to be," is insightfully descriptive of what is required of one who would be whole. In his book of the same title, he reminds us that the self-affirming life requires *will*: the will to have more life, to surpass ourselves. This sort of courage banishes everything cowardly; it is the opposite of submissiveness to external gods. Rather it affirms that which really is alive within, and is the will which compels the individual to take on difficult, but perfectly natural, life battles. It allows him to tackle the kind of small deaths which open him up to a larger life.

The death which belongs to life can take many forms, and is an aspect of growth and wholeness rarely examined. One of the most common forms of this death is sacrifice—the letting-go actions of what I call the small self: the ego, the petty, self-serving, self-interested self. These tiny deaths are required in order to be born into the real freedom life offers. "Die and Become," Goethe wrote. "Till thou hast learned this, Thou are but a dull guest on this dark planet."[1] The subject of sacrifice is one this book will turn to again and again, for it is a key to the actualized life: a universal law, if I might express it that way, for those who wish to express the truth within their very selves.

Finding out what we really want, and having the courage to be, do and have what we desire, requires facing the enemy within. This is difficult work for all but the most unusual person, and this is why the will is an essential ally. To face the enemy within means facing the obstacles and rejections of the outer world as we move toward what is real, toward what our real self wants. It means going against the wishes of those we love and may admire. It means leaving secure, comfortable ways of doing things to pursue something strange and frightening. It means facing our fears and hesitations, our desires for security, approval and rest—all natural objectives of the small self which wants guarantees, applause, and to be taken care of. Growing up means facing difficulties boldly.

Even children's fairy tales and mythology move this central message of what it means to be fully human into the deepest consciousness of our species. Fairy tales teach young children how to be courageous against evil and obstacles. They learn, sometimes before they can speak, what it means to stand up to their own fears. They learn from the stories they hear, before learning to read, that such tribulation is an integral part of growing up, and that this effort is to be expected. Stories teach, and I am convinced all children want to learn, that growth invariably brings with it conflict, dangerous experiences, demons that must be faced—dangerous and frightening if only because they are new, and because the child (and eventually the adult) doesn't know if he can master the situation.

Children learn that the currency for personal development is courage, perhaps also faith. They learn that they must face those conflicts squarely instead of running away. The stories they love most illustrate this lesson as well as teaching those virtues and attitudes needed for a whole, fearless life. When heroes and heroines stand up to bad wolves, angry, mean witches or evil kings and monsters, they emerge triumphant. Only in this way do they obtain that mysterious blessing which enables them to "live happily ever after."

As children learn to identify their different emotional selves with the characters and elements of each story, they also begin to understand what within them would lead them to ruin and what would lead them to a victorious, whole life.

Children also want to know "Whom do I want to be like?" as they identify with their storybook characters. Like adult philosophers, they intuitively start their "Who am I?" search in order to make their transition from childhood into adolescence and later into adulthood. They instinctively know that they'll be happy, strong and secure in the true sense of these words to the extent they can answer that most personal question and to the extent they can live out their answer in the real world of grown-ups and concrete, practical reality. Children are simultaneously inward-turning and outer-directed. They learn early what it is going to take to handle life. But since they are young and relatively helpless they sometimes choose to act in ways that will get them the approval and love they so desperately need. And this choice, although totally understandable, sets up a pattern of behaviors and strategies which doesn't always permit expression of their best selves. The child who passively accepts the criticism or abuse of a dominant parent, and who later finds it difficult to believe in his own self-worth, is an example of an early strategy which ultimately thwarts self-expression.

Inherent in the double-edged, knowledge/action requirement of wholeness is yet another idea: that there *is* a truth within the self which yearns to be known, and that the expression of this truth makes a person exist, be real, in her own eyes, ultimately in the eyes of others. The collective wisdom of mankind holds a deep and abiding belief in the idea that there is, within each person, some substantive truth waiting to be known, waiting to be expressed. When psychologists speak about someone as having an "authentic personality," they mean that the individual has managed to express what is most genuine, truthful and real about himself to others—in other words, that he has made *aliyah*.

Nietzsche linked human virtue to a person's ability to put the true self consciously into each deed. In his essay, "On Vir-

tue," he writes, ". . . that your very Self be in your action, as
the mother is in the child: let that be your formula of virtue."[2]
And the German mystic, Nicolas de Cusa, imagines that God
says to man, "Be thou thyself, and I shall be thine."[3] Again and
continually, the writings which would heal us, the teaching
which would make us strong, noble and whole, tell us that
growth, power and wholeness are obtained only through self-
knowledge, truthful expression, and the courage to act on what
we know to be real within ourselves. The teachings that mankind values most suggest that were we to actuate ourselves
through our choices and deeds, we would be worthy of receiving the blessings and attention of God himself.

From the earliest of times, many who embarked upon this
path achieved heroic, perhaps even saintly, status. Even if they
were thought to be madmen or heretics in their day, history
eventually rewarded them. Some who went their own way, listening to the voice within despite the tempting draw of a more
secure, comfortable, conforming existence, ultimately received
collective admiration.

Sir Thomas More, to cite one example, who lost his life
because he would not bless his king's marriage, was eventually
acknowledged as a Christian saint. Of him, playwright Robert
Bolt says, "Thomas More, as I wrote about him, became for
me a man with an adamantine sense of his own self. He knew
where he began and where he left off, what area of himself he
could yield to the encroachments of his enemies, and what to
the encroachments of those he loved. . . . What first attracted
me was a person who could not be accused of any incapacity
for life, who indeed seized life in great variety and almost
greedy quantities, and who nevertheless found something in
himself without which life was valueless and when that was denied him was able to grasp his death."[4]

In the last scene of *A Man for All Seasons*, a common man
comes to center stage to talk to the towns-people (and, by this

action, talks to the audience as well) after More's beheading.
He asks the onlookers, "I'm breathing. . . . Are you breathing
too? . . . It's nice, isn't it? It isn't difficult to keep alive, friends
. . . just don't make trouble—or, if you must make trouble,
make the sort of trouble that's expected."[5]

To find in ourselves what makes life worth living is risky
business, for it means that once we know we must seek it. It
also means that without it life will be valueless. More than just
a few find their most valued selves despite the risk, although
the majority seem to be (as in More's day) people who don't
wish to make any trouble—not even the kind that's expected.
The majority shrewdly stay dull to what in them is life and has
meaning. A few brave souls, however, do look within and are
so moved by what they find that they sacrifice, from then on,
whatever is necessary to bring that self into being.

Anyone who answers the yearning of the inner self is
called, has a vocation, in the original sense of that word, which
was "to be addressed by a voice." The clearest of such voca-
tions can, of course, be found in those who have a religious calling, or who are driven to express some form of genius. But I
believe that the word vocation should have a broader interpretation. Those who are called to find the law of their own being,
for example, who answer the call obediently, even if hesitat-
ingly, have a vocation. Those who sacrifice the things of this
world, the conventional way of living or perceiving things,
have a vocation. Anyone can be called—not just the religiously
inclined or the great gifted ones, since many of these may not,
in fact, be true to themselves as individuals.

Conscious assent to the inner voice and the subsequent alteration of life and world-view first requires a step back, a sort-
ing-out process, which I call social transcendence. Social
transcendence may develop spontaneously, as in the case of one
woman who told me she had always known she was different
and had always felt something within that guided her in one

direction or another. Or it could begin as a decision in one's teens, as it did for a man of eighty-eight who said that when he was just a boy of fifteen he looked around him at the other young boys in his community and at school, saw the way they were living, and decided right then that he was going to have something else, that there was something else within himself. He decided to hold himself to a stricter standard, to elevate his standard of living and make something out of his life as a whole.

In order to know what within is true and of most value, whenever these sorts of insights come, the individual detaches experientially from the rules, customs, belief systems, conventions and various idols of the external world. Social transcendence is a way to answer this inner call—be it a physical response (such as moving out of one's home, moving away from a hometown, or changing jobs, etc.) or just an emotional detachment from societal conventions and expectations as with a woman, let's say, who decides not to marry, not to have children, even though that is what she sees her friends doing and knows that that is what her family expects her to do. These kinds of detachment may be signs that an individual has begun the process of actualization.

Social transcendence is always growth-motivated—the person is growing into more of what he was meant to be, into more of what he already is. It is always a response to an inner call that has as its goal self-knowledge and truthful self-expression. It isn't a fear/anxiety motivated response to outer events. While the socially transcendent person may take conventional life very lightly because he is growing in conscious absorption with universally cherished and heartfelt values, his choices and behaviors are not anarchistic or anti-social. Even though on the surface it may appear as if the individual is backing away and losing interest in all the usual things, in the long run there develops a progressively cooperative, stewardly and morally concerned personality who is able to adopt a neatly balanced selfish/selfless life in relation to the world.

I think it interesting that Abraham Maslow acknowledged this phenomenon in a paper he presented in 1951, when he reported that his *healthiest* subjects were independent, detached and self-governing, and had a tendency to look within for their guiding values and for the rules by which they lived. He also observed their strong preference, even need, for privacy and their detachment from people in general. His healthiest subjects were only superficially accepting of social customs, while in private they were quite casual and even humorously tolerant of them, not feeling that conventions were very important to them. They had the ability to fight convention when they thought it necessary, and judged things by their own inner criteria. When they felt that something (about American culture, in the case of Maslow's study) was good, they accepted it. When they felt that something was bad, they rejected it. For all these reasons, Maslow called such people *autonomous*.

He meant by that word that these individuals were ruled by the laws of their own character, rather than by the laws of society. Lest we think that these persons would lead themselves and us into anarchy, it is helpful to note that throughout his writings Maslow suggests that only the healthiest personalities are capable of making choices in a way that they select what is probably good for them and good for all. For example, he says, "In these healthy people, we find duty and pleasure to be the same thing, as is also work and play, self-interest and altruism, individualism and selflessness. . . . Only to the self-disciplined and responsible person can we say, 'Do as you will, and it will probably be all right.' "[6]

Others also have reassuring words about values expressed by the choices of the healthy individual. The psychotherapist Clark Moustakas identifies a host of values he calls "universal values"—the values which collectively represent life, health and the consistently essential values of mankind: love, truth, freedom, beauty, justice, to name a few. These are the qualities which represent the good, and which give individual life (as well as relational life) its meaning, depth and stability. Moustakas calls the individual "authentic" who is "genuinely present, and present in such a way that his freedom is used responsibly; growth of his self is rooted in genuine existence, in justice, and in truth."[7]

Moustakas links self-betrayal (i.e., the fall from authenticity) to a failure to stay with universal values. I am convinced that as humans move into authentic, self-actuating relationships with themselves and others, they live out the good in a way that inspires and effects the good for all. It is only healthy personalities who have the strength and the will, for instance, to love their enemy, to do unto the other as they would be done unto. Only in those who have established a link between their own integrity and their choices do we see expressed the will to obey what is known to be the good, the honest, the true.

Social detachment involves a conversion of manners, to use a term from monastic literature—a term which will be explored more fully in the next chapter. Once an individual has answered the vocational call, everything in life is absorbed with—perhaps I should say sacrificed to—this journey; everything is given up (if gradually, incrementally, and with resistance) in favor of meeting the requirements of the call. In other words, the person undertakes a radical reinterpretation of day-to-day living, even—as we shall see—a radical reinterpretation of self. Yet this is always done in differing ways and degrees, depending on the person and the situation he is in at the time that the work most strenuously begins.

As mentioned only superficially in the introductory remarks, social transcendence can take place within the context of any life-style. While I sought out people who had physically detached themselves from urban and suburban living in order to conduct this research, I work with corporate clients on an on-going basis who clearly are the monk type. Their calling, as it were, is business. They are, for example, gifted in a particular field or another, and are as disciplined and committed to their work as a Trappist monk is to his.

While the degree of social transcendence differs, and while the degree of severity of sacrifice is as varied as the individuals themselves, there are some patterns of letting go held in common by all who are called to the vocation under discussion:

♦ *Sacrifice of* collective opinion, custom, vanity, security, guarantees, *in favor of* identifying and expressing the deepest values of one's life: love, truth, health, beauty, compassion, etc.
♦ *Sacrifice of* living unconsciously, of not knowing who one is or what is right *in favor of* bringing the law of one's being into existence through conscious expression.
♦ *Sacrifice of* direct and "safe" routes of accomplishment *in favor of* those which may be more demanding, risk-laden, ethical, illogical, unpopular, etc.
♦ *Sacrifice of* the individual's peculiar, risk-avoiding tendencies (e.g., withdrawal from or avoidance of difficulty) *in favor of* reliability, commitment, and responsibility in relationship to self-and-others.

Of course, the swing to the new perspective and way of conduct doesn't happen overnight. This journey takes many, many years. As one man of forty-eight admitted, having struggled to bring some of these behaviors about in his life for almost a decade, "When I realized what I had to do, I knew I was in for the work of my life. I knew it was going to take me years. I saw myself at the edge of the abyss, at the threshold of that which I didn't know how to be yet wanted to be. But I felt that even if the odds were a million to one, I could make it. Even if it took the rest of my life, I wanted to try. For I saw that without making the effort, I really had no life—not one that mattered anyway. So I just made up my mind that however long it took, I would do the work."

2

The First Step

I need so very little to live on. Having "things" just interests me less and less. I sleep when I'm tired, and not much more than four hours per night. I wear khaki trousers to all events, with or without a jacket. All of what I wear appears to fit into a chest of drawers. I eat very little. Conversation is more important than radio, TV, movies, etc. I am a solitary person and I read a great deal. [Study Participant and Businessman, Pennsylvania]

There are as many ways to answer the call for an inward journey as there are persons called. Therefore, it is helpful to see if a pattern can be found in the structure and life-organization of those who, for all intents and purposes, have pulled away from conventional ways.

For those who enter a formal religious monastery, life is organized in minute detail. Traditions, the rituals and philosophical tenets of their belief system, the very necessity of integrating one life with many lives in a smooth running fashion, creates a structured, corporate environment with most major decisions taken care of by policies, customs, dietary practices and use of time. All the minor trivia of day-to-day living and worship are tightly organized for the monasterial citizen. The great religious traditions of the world have given us examples of what these organized approaches to the inward journey are

25

like. Almost every major religion has had its group of devotees who withdrew from conventional life in order to live a discipleship in the deepest way possible within the context of their own faith.

Monastic life and the organization which encouraged such a life precedes Christianity. In Hinduism, for example, isolated caves, mountain tops and ashrams have been home for religious men, either singly or in groups. Here they practice their arduous yogic and meditative prayers so as to experience *samahdi:* that state of superconscious awareness of identity with God. A Zen Buddhist enters a monastery for the same reason: to see and experience his highest reality, the truth of his own being, within the structure of the monastery. In early Judaism, the monks of Qumran lived in devoted consciousness of Old Testament prophecy. Christianity (specifically—but not exclusively—Catholicism) has the same, centuries-old tradition: the monk's aim is to iive out his faith according to the example and Gospel of Christ, to join in mysterious union with him.

However monasteries may differ in their religious traditions, each structures life tightly for its residents so that they can attain basically the same goal: to merge into closer union with God, as he is defined by them, and, in striving for that goal, to retreat from worldly activity and life as others around them customarily live it. All increase their solitude, silence, and the orderliness of their life. Thomas Merton once wrote that the monk is not defined by his task, or by his usefulness. The monk lives in order to concern himself with life itself, not to exercise a specific function. This outlook certainly sums up the lives of those who would be monks: that they respond to that within themselves which is life, truth, love and attempt, through each action, choice and day's living to embody that.

In Catholicism, the term for the practical adjustments and sacrifices by which monks alter their daily life is "conversion of manners." Through a variety of vows and obediences, monks develop stability in their practice and in their faith. Vows like poverty, chastity, silence and service alter a monk's personal interests, sensuality, even his freedom to come and go as desired; these all are subordinated to the authority of tradition, to elders, to God.

In the silence and simplicity of their lives, monks learn to listen to the persistent voice of discontent within themselves. By abandoning worldly distractions, by assuming a conversion of manners, their newly structured life forces them into intimate and growing relationship with their inner voice. Their absorption with this voice, their heightened listening powers, is not usually possible in the distracting environment of the world. Their various vows help cultivate and strengthen a deep posture of inner awareness.

By contrast, the socially transcendent individual has no ready-made daily routine, no like-minded others with whom to associate. Because there is no concrete blueprint for organizing a secular life dedicated to becoming more unique (i.e., which involves having more time to think, reflect, study, and commune with Self), each must necessarily design his own structure.

As we will see, it is not just by taking formal vows or by living within the strict rules of a monastery that people break with conventional life. Sometimes their awareness and ability to detach from that life just happens as a perceptual shift, a mental objectivity, a lifting-out of the normal way of seeing and relating to the interpersonal/social reality in which life is lived.

One man described his perceptual shift in this way: "I've had the ability to observe myself in society at large for a long time. I've seen myself constantly able to view things in the bigger picture. I know I spend more time conceptualizing about life in general, while at the same time seeing myself as an actor in the activity I'm watching. Your questions, for example, were easy for me to answer because these are the kinds of large issue questions that I've thought about for a long time. I'd say that what separates me from the norm is my ability to conceptualize in this way—to stand back and see things as whole, while continuing to watch myself."

Anyone who develops this critical, objective, and conceptual sense in relation to society can, in the broadest sense, be called a monk. I agree with Merton who suggests that social movements—such as the hippies, the civil rights movement, the peace movement—and all those individuals who became interested in spiritual disciplines such as Yoga or Zen have aspects that can be called monastic. These social and individual tendencies imply a radical break with ordinary life and social patterns. Says Merton, "They have their asceticism, their 'discipline,' in the various kinds of sacrifices they make in order to 'break with their own past,' with their own normal milieu, with the society of parents, or with the social order with which they violently disagree. . . . They represent an attitude toward the world which is analogous to that of the monk.[1]

However, this objectivity with respect to conventional life has its problems. For one thing, a sense of meaninglessness can develop for the *uninvolved,* those who find themselves always onlookers. The need to create meaning (i.e., perhaps *new* meanings where old ones prove pointless) increases as people pull back from the things which other people find meaningful. Another perhaps more practical concern is simply that of structuring daily life. Because a common goal of all those in this study was a desire to have more time and fewer demands from trivial activities, people showed themselves capable of tremendous creativity, in some cases frugality, in the way they met their financial and time-management goals. Unlike the monk, they have no pre-set daily schedule to follow. Thus, they must locate their own practical solutions to a variety of problems: how to work while still having time for other activities, for example. This is a key issue for the secular monk who usually is not financially independent and must continue to support himself. Previous interpersonal commitments (e.g., to spouse, children, friends) who might be dependent on them for economic or emotional support is another practical consideration. Simplifying life becomes yet another element to deal with since the social transcendent person usually wants to carve out more time for reflection, study or just inactivity, "non-doing" as in the Zen tradition. Certainly each solves these puzzles in his own way. Yet strong similarities exist, enough to discuss some of the common patterns found among study participants. Whatever the outer form of life, each lives in such a way as to become more conscious of the Self within. Some manage this by living completely alone, others by dividing time between two residences, others by separating themselves from family and friends in a systematic way. The frugal and judicious use of time, money and other resources was another common denominator. Also evident was the continual defining and redefining of self in relation to the world.

I should mention at this point that there seemed to be two types of reality the study participants were dealing with and trying to integrate. The first has been called "the transpersonal" (or superconscious, or true Self, or higher Self—in other words the deepest aspects of the whole personality). The second type of reality I would call the interpersonal/social level of reality, and of course this deals with the self in relation to others, the environment, the social order of things. What seems to happen initially, as individuals desire to understand and deepen their bond with their transpersonal reality (i.e., all the various aspects of themselves: their dream world, their feelings, their various physiological tendencies and the unique demands of their own nervous systems, etc.), is that they pull back from the interpersonal level of reality. Eventually, as we shall see in later chapters—especially in the chapter that deals with the stewardship pattern—it is clear that the interpersonal branch of reality begins to change for the socially transcendent person. In the later, more mature phase of actualization the individual is able to relate to other-and-environment in a more generous, caring way. At first, however, much like a child needs nurturing from its mother, the individual needs to be self-nurturing, and this is where the pulling-back, detaching takes place.

This pulling-away stage can last many years as the transpersonal level of reality begins to be clarified and strengthened. Not only do individuals *think* differently about themselves, but they also begin to view themselves, experience themselves, as *acting* differently. Their choices and acts start to honor their more clarified and most cherished values. It is as if a higher faculty of the self (probably this is why spiritual psychologists and theologians have called this the "Self") comes into being—through awareness, the will, through choices and acts—and this aspect of the personality energizes the individual's ability to know himself, to act on what he knows.

Summing up this altered way of knowing and behaving by the word *obedience* might help clarify a cluster of changed actions during this first phase of social/self transcendence. I mean by obedience that the individual *wills* that which accomplishes his highest objectives. Obedience is submitting to authority. Of course, within the framework of the traditional monk's solution (i.e., residing in and membership in a cloistered, religious community), obedience to authority may be more easily defined, observed and understood. However, for socially transcendent persons there isn't someone "out there" (i.e., in the home, organization, community, or church) telling them to be obedient to this rule or that policy. Rather it is they themselves who desire something more, who desire the goals their inner self only vaguely whispers. These individuals learn to listen carefully to their inner authority as a way of saving their integrity and their very lives.

Of this goal, one man said, "My work, as I see it now, is just to hear what the Self is, hear what it wants me to do. I would also say that a person's growth in this way, the level of receptivity to the directives of one's own being, is the most important contribution we can make to the world, because these directives are always healing."

Thus, for the socially—and self—transcendent person, authority rests in the truth or law of the developing higher Self. This poses problems since such a law is not only hard to grasp—being often just a subjective feeling, sense or stirring within—but in the beginning phases it is also changeable, tinged with conflicting emotions. The phrase used by psychiatrist R.D. Laing, "experiential anarchy," comes to mind as a sound one for describing the earliest stages of trying to locate this internal authority.

One woman, who wrote to me asking to join the research group, epitomizes the inner anarchy which makes specific directives so hard to pin down and comprehend. She wrote, "I filled out your questionnaire yesterday, put it in the envelope, sealed it, and then ripped open the envelope and made additions and corrections, was about to go to sleep, ripped it open again, made some more additions, slashed out a bunch of stuff and sealed it up again. This morning I got up, opened it again, read it over and threw it in the fire. I had to conclude that I'm really not the type of person you're looking for. You see, I'm doing what I'm doing, but I'm not sure why. I uprooted myself from the east coast last year when my youngest son (of five children) was accepted at college, and I could finally do what I wanted to do—quit my boring job and go to the California coast which I've always loved, to live by myself for the first time in my life. . . . I've been doing this for a year. . . . Being on the spot as far as declaring a philosophy of life really threw me. . . . I simply am unable to come to any definitive conclusions."

Because I sensed that this woman was in the early throes of pulling back—a phase that is often disjointed, incoherent, and disturbingly non-conforming—I wrote her a note saying just that. Soon I received another letter:

"You're right. I'm on an incoherent journey fostered by faith and trust. In fact, I think my entire life could be described that way. I think what upset me so much about your questionnaire was that I was forced to admit this to myself. When stable people ask me questions about my background I have a regular spiel which I rattle off, putting everything into a cohesive pattern, and I've done this so often that I believed it myself. Psychologically sound people, I was taught, have structure and purpose. They know what they're doing. The only people who know me as I really am are my children. I can be thoroughly honest with them because I know they'll love me no matter what I do. I knew you were looking for true responses to your questions, and I couldn't do it because I had never done it before. Strange."

Her remarks are repeated in one way or another by most people in the study who find themselves in hard to understand life-situations, especially in the early stages of their actualization process.

Fortunately, as time goes by, the demands of the Self are easier to hear. This is especially true when life becomes well-ordered and simplified, for the general rule is this: as the external life gets simplified and less distractive, the inner life is strengthened and developed. If anything, pulling away from conventional life, *because* withdrawing is rooted in a sincere desire to be true to oneself, forces the individual to face the inner struggle and the inner self which wants to surface. It is through hearing—and obeying—the demand to make a life-adjustment that the *ability* to face oneself grows. In fact, as will be described in the next chapter, many abilities grow along with self-trust and with the bond-to-Self. As each correction is made, the bond between self and Self grows stronger, thus giving more power to the voice of the Self, more clarity of purpose to the individual's life.

"I was burdened by the weight of an inner vision of myself as an ignorant man, cowardly and afraid," one man said of his increased sense of what was required of him. "I was nearly broken by the knowledge that I had to change my life myself, that I alone had to develop a closer affinity to God—that is to say, to Self, to Life, to the Tao, the Great Unnamable. I had to set it up so that that affinity could develop. My work was well-defined once that awareness existed."

The first thing that occurs is an awareness that something in one's customary way of living doesn't work, isn't health-promoting, isn't life-supporting. This initial awareness is experienced in various ways and at different times and isn't unusual even in the general population. What *is* unusual is that socially transcendent individuals *do* something, alter their lives, as a result of their awareness, in such a way that furthers the development of the person they sense they could be. Some people said they wanted time to sort things out. Still others described how marital problems or some personal disillusionment at home, at work or with world concerns gave the impetus to the initial awareness. Whatever the stimulus, that special light which comes with the knowledge that they must change helps people see things differently, helps them identify specifically what actions to take as next steps in their own development.

All those I spoke to had a highly personal realization which propelled them to take the first step in pulling away from the mainstream of living. One bright and sensitive man said, "In 1970 I saw a copy of the *Whole Earth Catalogue*, and it presented a whole new realm of possibilities to me. I saw a picture of the earth, riding in its finite little orb. That's what influenced me to pull away from the way in which others around me were living. The underlying philosophy that we have to take care of this fragile little planet was a challenge to my life. It made sense, and from then on I had the desire to figure out a lifestyle for myself that was consistent with that in every detail."

Another, a woman, reported something quite different. She and her husband both realized at about the same time that they needed to improve the quality of their daily lives, and that they wanted to increase the time they spent together. "We wanted better, more natural surroundings, fresh air and water. I *need* trees, hills, greater independence, more natural sights, sounds, and smells. I want to grow my own food. I want to learn as long as I live, and this new life we've designed is a way of fulfilling those needs. For my husband, our move was imperative since his health demanded it."

A young man, a former Olympic athlete, said of his urban life, "I found living in the city all week was unproductive. It sapped my strength in a way. What I needed was time out, time alone, time to reflect in a more solitary way what to do with my life. I needed more silent surroundings. I wanted to get away from the demands of my wife's career."

What all these people have in common is the ability to discern what they need and make appropriate life adjustments to accommodate those needs. All intuitively and specifically knew what elements they wanted to alter in life in order to live more honestly. It is as if some new faculty or power develops within—a critical thinking/observing faculty which allows them to watch, editorialize, and know concretely what to do in their day-to-day living in order to be authentic and whole.

For a few, this awakening—if I may call the detached perception by that name—came early in life. For others the feeling gradually grew that something more was necessary in life in order for meaning, purpose and wholeness to exist. One man in his seventies reported that he had made the break with conventional living in midlife. He said that he had wanted to live in a way that permitted him to become more God-centered. "I pulled away from the world through a desire to have more time for study, meditation, and prayer, and to search for a less violent way of life," he said.

A woman in her sixties said she knew early in life what she needed: "As a very young woman, I saw myself able to extricate myself from some inordinately tough situations. I knew I was my own person, that I deserved to live in my own way. I felt myself become more secure within during those early days, and with this security came further detachment. I trusted my judgment about things and realized that my own unique perceptions were valid for me—valid enough for me to act on. These would provide me with the directions I'd need all my life."

I should say a few words here about the type of person in my study. As mentioned briefly in the introduction, I ran my ad requesting volunteers for the study in rural newspapers and in one national journal which reaches both urban and rural readers. Most of the people in my study were either self-employed or retired. Only a few were financially affluent. Therefore almost all had to be ingenious in coming up with a way of earning money in order to support themselves while they took some time off for thinking, reflecting, living in sparsely populated communities. Some worked part-time. Some lived on almost nothing (e.g., two participants volunteered the information that they lived on less than five thousand dollars per year; another—a young woman—hinted that she lived on very little but didn't say how much). In no case did I ask people how much they earned, nor did I ask their ages. Many were uncomfortable with this latter omission, and asked me why I didn't ask. When I replied that my ad simply asked for people *over* thirty-five years of age, and that age in and of itself didn't mean anything for this study (or perhaps I should add that it means little to me, as do other categories into which social scientists like to put people), they seemed satisfied. Several men worked as carpenters, lived in cabins they had built themselves (or in cooperative communities in which everyone pooled their resources, lived very simply, and rented cabins very inexpensively), and some worked sometimes, saved up their money, then took time off for contemplation and rest.

Whatever their financial situations, the timing of their initial awareness that a change was needed, or the motives which prompted their life adjustments, the desire to think, study, and reflect more, the yearning to pray or to live in more natural settings, repeatedly came up as goals. The superordinate goal seemed the same: obedience to the law of each person's higher nature.

3

Practical Considerations

Being alone is very helpful and ordering to me. My
desk, for example, is a symbolic way for me to organize
my life. I clear it as a way of structuring myself. I live
simply, without electricity, flush toilet, hot water, or recent model car. I have not had offspring, or done the
usual family thing. My main work is helping improve
the world and serving people. [Study Participant and
Environmentalist, California]

To obey the inner authority, people must devise practical, day-
to-day ways to restructure their lives. There are obligations to
meet, regardless of the individual's financial situation. One
may have plenty of money, but may have business interests to
manage. Another may have children or a spouse to support—
emotionally and in other ways. Yet another may be retired and
have enough money and freedom to do as he pleases, but may
have health problems to contend with, problems which con-
strict freedom in ways unknown before. Each person in this
study was different and thus had a unique set of challenges in
front of him which had to be faced in order to create a new life.
However, common threads were very apparent.

Everyone said they used money and other resources (e.g.,
food, transportation vehicles, community services) more
wisely. I recall an interview with one man, a person of consid-
erable means and financial security, who was surprised to hear

that not everyone in the study was affluent. He had assumed, as many do, that in order to have the courage and ability to take on the so-called "higher" needs of the personality, people had to be financially secure. In fact, that doesn't seem to be the case. They have to *feel* secure before facing the work, but that is another matter.

What must exist in order to carve out a unique and personally meaningful life is *high self-esteem,* that strong underpinning of self-trust and self-worth which says, "I can do all things if I really put my mind to it." Or, "Even when I don't know what to do in a situation, I know I'll be able to figure out what to do eventually." A bit of this quality must be present in all who would tackle the really hard battles of life. But just a little is all that's required since taking on the battles fuels the self-esteem even when the battles themselves are lost. It is enough for people just to know they were willing to stand up and fight for something they believed in, valued or cared about. Having said this, I should add that everyone in the study was quite frugal with money: both those that had little of it and those that had a great deal.

Time, not money, seemed to be the element most coveted for the new life. This was especially true for those who still work or who had spent many years working at an eight-to-five job, and hadn't yet integrated work into the "work is play" idea and tasks of the more well-developed self-actualized personality. The work as play attitude, as we shall see in the chapter on stewardship, is simply that balanced and quite constructive solution which comes when people do what they enjoy or are most naturally suited to do. In this way the individual gets pleasure out of day-to-day work tasks because these are the intrinsic expressions of the unfolding personality (as opposed to externally imposed tasks which come out of doing work one feels one "should" do).

To claim more time for personal use, people scaled down

their involvement with the world of things, with obligatory but perhaps unsatisfying social activities, and in this way they enhanced their ability to protect themselves from things they simply didn't wish to do. I think this objective is summed up nicely by what author and researcher Duane Elgin calls "voluntary simplicity." In his book of the same name, Elgin describes a way of life that is outwardly simple and inwardly rich. He makes a strong sociological and environmental case for such a lifestyle, and my impression is that all of the study subjects have designed such a life for themselves.

One woman said, "I've simplified my life so that I'll have time for the things I really want to do. I want time to think, to read, to walk more. I want time for rewarding encounters with others. Simplifying outer things lets me order my interior life. I now spend a good deal of every day walking in the woods, making pottery, gardening and writing. I'm more clearminded, and I believe I'm growing into a better, more responsible, even a nicer person."

Eager to share his new discovery, another man said, "I've pared down my life incredibly. When I left my full-time involvement with a business venture, I vowed that I'd never work for anyone else again. I wanted more time to do what I knew to be important to me. I told myself it would be O.K. to work part-time, and that's exactly what I've arranged. This works for me because I'm involved in a structured setting, with definite hours three days a week, which I need—never having had so much free time on my hands before. Then, the rest of the week, I have entirely to myself, to use as I please. As it turns out, I've chosen to get up early, regardless of the day, go to sleep early too. I don't want to waste the time sleeping or watching television. I eat very simply, and I've given or thrown away most of the possessions that were just gathering dust."

Describing her life in yet another way, a woman from the midwest said, "My routine is stable. I don't do anything that seems pointless or boring. I don't waste money or time on things I don't need. I've separated myself from the way other people do things in that I'm not a joiner. I don't drink or smoke or take drugs. I read, think and write more than I believe most people do. I'd guess I give away more money than average. It goes to my church or to my children who are still young and struggling. What I give is peanuts since my income isn't large. Yet, I always have extra. I don't yearn for expensive things. And I always have enough to spend, save or just give away."

A sculptor, deeply absorbed in a new direction his pottery was taking, asked to be "excused" from filling out the rather lengthy research questionnaire. Instead, he requested an in-person interview to be held after his normal working day. "I just don't wish to give that much prime time to writing out these answers," he said, "since writing doesn't come too easily for me. But I'm sure I can tell you what you need to know in person if you can manage to interview me in the evening when my mind is not absorbed with my work."

Married people in the study reported many innovative ways to deal with their individual needs for solitude, privacy and growing desire to alter social activity. In some cases, couples intentionally separated during the workweek and spent weekends together. In other cases, guest houses and separate quarters were established to give each person privacy and time alone. In most cases, marriage didn't stop just because one or both parties wanted to be alone. This seemed especially true in those relationships where both people are reflective, quiet types and where they crave the same developmental results.

One married woman described her solution for obtaining quiet time as follows: "I take time each day when my husband is away from the house to sit quietly. This turns out to be quite a lot of time—about three hours or more usually. When he's home, it's still easy to spend time exactly as I want to: thinking, reading, contemplating. He's quiet too, and he wants time for just about the same things. He spends time in his study which is rather large and is almost like a separate apartment. I sit here in the dining room and look at the ocean for long stretches of time. My thoughts are usually on spiritual subjects now, not on community matters or on gossip. That's just not the current flow of thoughts I have these days. When there's another person in the house, I go into my bedroom and shut the door. I really don't like having house guests any more. We've cut way back on that. We've even pulled away from our children, and I believe they're pleased to see us as self-sufficient adults with a life of our own. Somehow when we do get together our relationship is stronger."

"I have a good marriage," disclosed another woman, a wife and mother of two children whose husband lived and worked in another city for four days of the week. "For the last fifteen years, my husband and I have chosen to live apart during a portion of the week. We met in high school, and it was love at first sight. At least it was for me. For him, it was bewilderment. We dated until our early twenties, got married, had a daughter a year and a half later, and soon decided we wanted to move out of Los Angeles. So we bought a camper, and for almost a year lived in that camper—the two of us, our daughter and a dog. Our second child was conceived in that camper. I must say we both enjoyed every bit of that travel experience, and we'll return to that way of life when we retire. But now we have different requirements.

"From Monday through Thursday, my husband lives in San Francisco where he works. I stay here with the children. That way he gets to do the things he wants without my having to do them, and I do what I want. I credit our strong marriage to this arrangement. Even my son has told me that all he hears at school is how the parents of his friends argue. 'Mom, you and dad never fight,' he told me last week. It really felt great to know our son realizes we have something special."

A man who characterized himself as highly competitive, and who said he loved structure, described his marital arrangement which gives him two days a week to stay at his rural retreat home: "I wanted to uncouple myself from the demands of my wife's work, and it turned out that this solution worked for her too. I suppose you could even say we've switched roles. My wife is a physician who gets up before dawn. By five in the morning, she's out jogging with the dog. I don't see her until eight at night, and by then I've fixed dinner. I take care of the day-to-day decisions so that she doesn't have to. I even buy her clothes, and I think I do it pretty well, actually, because I have good taste. We enjoy having uninterrupted time to ourselves to read, think, reflect, so we separate during a part of the week. I also have to structure the rest of my time pretty carefully because of my time away from home and that makes me very purposeful. I don't like my time frivolously taken up by phone conversations or social things, even though of course I do all of that—it's just that by slicing out a piece of the week for myself, I'm able to do less of the trivial things and more of what I consider essential."

Almost all, married or unmarried, with children or without, said they wanted to do what was important to *them*, even if it meant others might think them selfish. Many realized that by preserving their strength and by cultivating their new sense of purpose, they would, in the long run, be better equipped to serve others. As one woman, a wife and a mother of two grown children, put it, "I feel that a person who says 'Yes' to all requests becomes a scattered personality. I simply cannot serve those I would serve if I'm pulled in all directions at once. So, what looks like selfishness to some is at the root a selfless thing."

As described in the last chapter, creating the new life demands obedience, and in the case of the secular monk it is obedience to an inner authority. In order to penetrate a larger truth and to give life meaning one must ultimately surrender the comfortable ways of doing things, the habitual ways of responding to life. Perhaps most difficult is the matter of letting go of what others think, of the approval and even the love of others. Many spoke, often with poignant and lingering sadness, of parents, ex-spouses or friends who couldn't accept them in their newly chosen lives, or with whom they could no longer communicate.

"My brother," explained one young man who had quit school after high school and was working on and off as a carpenter, "is a very successful businessman, extremely involved with making money. He cannot understand why I live like this—it makes no sense to him, and of course most of the time I don't understand it myself, so it's hard for me to explain it. It's not a logical thing at all, and when I feel myself having to justify myself I pull back even more."

A young woman, whose father is a chemical engineer and who lost her mother while still in college, decided after college that she wanted to live in a rural area. She moved with a boyfriend to California. First she found a job as a waitress, saving her money diligently. Next she found some acreage, overlooking the ocean, purchased that, and finally built her own home—alone. Instead of acknowledging her actions as an achievement, her father withdrew.

"My father still wishes I would live out the American Dream," she says. "You know, marry, have kids, live in the suburbs. He can't understand my life. In fact, I think it makes him uncomfortable. He did come to visit me once, with his new wife. I was really looking forward to their visit and prepared for it, thinking they'd stay a few days. I mean, they did drive all the way out from the east coast. But they came in, looked around at my little cabin, and I could see it was a strain for them to imagine my living here. They stayed for lunch and then left. I've felt badly about it, but there's nothing I'm going to do differently. I can't *not* live this way. I've always felt I had to be true to myself, and I act on that regardless of the consequences."

A woman in her sixties told of her alienation from community norms: "I live in a small town, and my family has always belonged to the same church. You have to understand that in this town, which epitomizes small town, Southern Baptist culture, people know about your business, and they have a comment about everything. My family always belonged to a certain church, and so did I, and so did my six children. But in the 1960's I began to realize that the church was avoiding its responsibilities in the civil rights area. It seemed to me that the Christian position was not being taken by the church—at least that's how I saw it, and of course these matters are very personal ones. For my part, I could not in good conscience continue going to and supporting a church that didn't meet my criteria for Christian conduct. So I formally withdrew myself, and my children, from membership in that church. I'm not sure if you realize what it means in a small, southern town to do that. The action I took was one which required all the courage I had. As I look back on it now I see that what I did made me grow in my own eyes. But living through that decision, and my subsequent actions, was one of the hardest things I've ever done."

Sometimes decisions like these, or others which involve a totally different set of circumstances and choices, look as though the individual may not be meeting his social or family responsibilities. The person, for example, who quits a secure and promising career in order to locate more satisfying, truthful work might be viewed as a laggard, as unambitious, or as irresponsible. As we have seen, family and friends can be rejecting when they don't understand or cannot accept the changes they observe. But in a very real way it is most frightening for the individual undergoing and engineering such changes, and were it not for some inward sense that the change must be made they would probably not find the courage to make it. This is why it is necessary for individuals to develop their will. The German mystic, Meister Eckhardt, reminds us that love has its being only in our will. "The man who has more will, he also has more love."[1] As a person develops his or her love for the Self, he simultaneously finds the will to do what is most difficult.

Many study respondents spoke of fears that cropped up when they had to face unknown situations, lack of money and security and disapproval of family and friends. Said one, "I have to say I feel a lack of integration when I'm faced with uncertain conditions, as opposed to greeting the unknown with more faith, more confidence. Of course, I *do* greet it and I continue along this path. But I don't mind telling you that I get scared along the way."

Another said, "I've had to face the things which I've been afraid of most—my own abyss, if I can put it that way. But knowing what I was, knowing what I had to do, I realized that even if there was only one chance in a million that I could make it, I'd have to give it a try. There was no life for me otherwise."

The youngest person in the study, a woman of twenty-seven and a single mother living in a remote region of Nova Scotia, described her battles with insecurity: "I've made a commitment to live by and work with my creative energy, pursuing a spiritual path. This is how I want my life to be . . . but I'd have to say I'm not secure in all of this. I feel as if this is my home in the 'wilderness,' and 'desert,' and so I just have faith in this process. Sometimes, though, I feel very vulnerable. I try to search inwardly for guidance, try to be sensitive to what I'm led to do. I'm not as good as this sounds, not always successful or disciplined, so I must stress the 'try' part of my answer. I came here because I love the beauty, the silence, the depth of where I live. I want to go deeper—I'm breaking new ground, alone."

We know exploration is a less important need than that for safety. We know, for example, that only the person who feels inwardly confident, who has a certain degree of faith in his or her ability to meet the unknown, can venture forth. The two individuals quoted above, for example, are not affluent. The young woman from Nova Scotia organized a day-school so as to support her young child and herself. The man who said he feels a lack of integration when he faces the unknown is currently working as a maintenance man for a development company he doesn't really like. This type of exploration takes special skills, skills which come with the greater bonding to and trust of the Self.

One of those I interviewed—the sculptor who asked to have an interview rather than responding to the written questionnaire—said this about his self-trust: "I never pull an answer out of myself. It just comes as I have the need. The need to know something prompts the response from within me. If I have a need, I have a sense of confidence in myself that I can fill that need. That's the way I communicate with myself—the need produces the answers. I trust myself . . . my self-talk is supportive. It's easy for me to love myself. I'm really quite a good person, even though I suppose I have my flaws. I respond as honestly as I can to situations, I don't have a lot of anger or prejudices in me, I've never intentionally hurt anyone, and I've experienced more difficulty than most people and survived it. I suppose that's why I trust myself."

The ability to face the conflicts and fears within ourselves, to acknowledge our longing for security, for roots and unending love and approval and yet—at the same time—to remain unswervingly fixed on an uncertain, insecure path because we sense it to be our right path, is, to my way of thinking, a heroic thing. This is the courage to be. Thomas Merton says of the monk who confronts his own challenges squarely, "The paradox that one must face, if he really takes the truth seriously, is the pragmatic fact that sincerity means insecurity."[2]

To sustain the weight of freedom, even to make a truly free choice, is something only the actualizing person *can* do. To live in such a way that we yield up anything that interferes with the truth of our being is an entirely different way of life than is customary for the average person. Yet, the actualizing person demonstrates the ability to choose the more truthful option in many tangible daily choices, as we have seen in the personal examples given in this chapter. Repeatedly, the actualizing person acts out of a detached view of society—and often out of a more objective view of self—even when those actions create discomfort, fears, and unpopular outcomes. Again and again, the actualizing person sacrifices short-term security for the long-term integration and truthful expression of life.

Ultimately, of course, what is sacrificed is one's separateness, the personal small self. This is the great paradox of this particular developmental route: that as the self becomes more and more unique, original, perhaps idiosyncratic, a larger world-view, a more unified perspective and greater universality, is expressed. Almost all in the study commented on the fact that although they had started their journey by drawing back into themselves, they found themselves growing back toward others in a more contributive, helping, supporting way. The artists in the group wanted to create, so as to share their creations with others. The peace activities became more community-minded. One man, a financial advisor, expressed it this way: "I feel I need to move out of my quiet, private, rather independent shell to work more closely with others. I feel that I would like to teach more, extend myself more. I don't know why I'm doing this since it's really quite inconvenient, and I'm pushing myself out of my areas of comfort. It's not logical, because much of what I find myself doing is irritating to me: more crowds, more traffic jams, a tighter schedule. But I feel a need to do it anyway."

Our next chapter will examine the pull of the stewardship pattern more thoroughly. Suffice it to say at this point that as actualization develops, the individual knows himself to be a part of an integrated, whole world and desires to function effectively and responsibily as a part of that whole. This motivational thrust—what Maslow termed "metamotivation"—has an entirely different base than participating in work or community projects because others expect it, or because of self-aggrandizing motives.

What we see then, in reviewing just some of the practical considerations faced by the socially transcendent person, is that out of a self-imposed ordeal grows new life-meaning, a revitalized way of being in the world, and a cluster of aptitudes or skills which allow the individual, in varying degrees, to venture forth as a mature, interrelated member of society. Among many abilities which appear to develop, the following seem particularly worth mentioning.

♦ The ability to reinterpret the self more truthfully in the context of a whole world-view: individuals alter their way of seeing themselves, the way they relate to others, work and community. They know and live out their values, with or without the approval of others, and begin to integrate inner and outer aspects of their lives in a consistent manner.

♦ The ability to manage resources—time, money, community services, etc.—creatively and efficiently. The individual starts to control the various resources of life rather than being at the effect of them.

♦ The ability to let go of conventional pressures for achievement, material goods, status symbols in favor of more intrinsically meaningful things, activities and goals. This renunciation, as we have seen, encompasses a wide range of attitudes and beliefs and entails a conscious and deliberate denial of things (material possessions, relationships, abstract ideas, values) which might fragment or render impotent the newly developing self and bond with Self.

◆ An ability to tolerate more ambiguity, change and not-knowing. The individual develops the strength—or skill—of living with fewer guarantees, and is able to put up with more insecurity. This is accompanied by growing openness to the true self, to one's own ability to find solutions, even when these aren't readily available.

◆ The ability to merge self-and-other interests. By this I mean that the necessary balance between selfish/selfless choices begins to emerge. Almost all I spoke with said that they were selfish people. At the same time each described his favorite activities in words that valued service, others, nature, caring, relationships and so on. There was a neat blending of inner/outer realities, a way of gently coming to terms and being receptive to the needs of the environment, or of others, as a high pleasure. The sense of separateness begins to dissolve as this perception/attitude grows. The woman who said she needed time to restore herself in order to have the strength to care for others is an example of this blending of selfish/selfless value. A young man who works as a carpenter six months of the year so that he can take the other six months to leisurely go bird-watching and walk in the forest is another example. A sculptor who purposes all his work as giving is yet a third illustration of this attitude.

◆ Creative problem-solving skills grow with the increase in self-awareness and the heightened communication with Self. The individual is able to really "see" the concrete problem in front of him without inordinate fears or other emotions clouding the brain's problem-solving mechanism. He confronts the present in fresh terms, not as a repetition of previous moments or out of habitual, mechanistic responses. Improvisation and spontaneous behaviors seem to grow out of the ability to see more clearly what needs to be done in a given situation.

Not one person I spoke to lacked problems to solve. However those in the study solved their problems in an innovative way. The example of married couples who wanted time alone, yet wanted to stay married, comes to mind. Nowhere in the media or popular wisdom had I come across the idea of consciously designed "time-out" (except in the case of dual-career couples who, for the most part, resist the idea of living or working in two separate locations). The people I interviewed were consistently able to obtain what they needed from others (i.e., from their environment, their work, their friends, etc.) while simultaneously protecting their privacy and while being helpful to others. In other words, there didn't appear to be an exploitive or manipulative edge to their problem-solving styles.

The actualizing person develops a world-view analogous to that of the most disciplined, devout monk. He or she makes a radical break with ordinary life as we know it, certainly perceptually—as in the case of my business clients who continue to live and work "as if" they were a part of the mainstream of society, but who are emotionally detached to a high degree—and probably also in a physical sense too as in the case of this study's participants. The radical perceptual/physical break is made in order to obey an inner dictate to live truthfully and in order to live a more conscious, responsible and faithful life. To remain receptive to the nature and directives of the inner voice takes the same courage, discipline and sincerity as if one was a religious devotee. In almost all cases, the break made with conventional life is costly. And in *all* cases, the detached perception—of course, ultimately this *is* the break—is expensive since every bit of reality comes under scrutiny, and also because the individual begins to experience his truths and correct his life according to those inner realities, rather than continue living under—and responding to—the seductive perceptual screen of collective beliefs and opinions. People see themselves as they are—not as their egotistical self or idealized image would have them be, and this too is painful when what they are turns out to be so much less than what they would be. In the long run, however, it is out of this clear perspective that growth and self-respect emerge. For the short term though, especially in the early stages of social transcendence, there is a steep price to be paid.

The work, if it is to be done at all, must be done alone. And this ultimately is the threat of beginning such a process. The socially transcendent person is en route to becoming a minority-of-one: an authentic personality in a conforming world. Unlike the religious monk, who receives a ready-made life structure and even a good measure of social approval, the socially transcendent individual can be and can feel very much alone, cut off from familiar sources of love and belonging.

Fortunately, there are compensating benefits. Not the least of these is an expanding and increased ability to feel and express love in the truest and most generous sense of the word, as well as an enriched capacity to experience the self as part of an interrelated, whole world.

In other words, the individual—to the extent he becomes an individual, becomes actualized—loses the sense of separateness which is at the core of all anxiety, anxiety which signals the unlived, thwarted life. In our next chapter we will explore some of the manifestations of the authentic personality as it expresses its mature and caring love through work. For it is through their work and through their interpersonal activities that actualizing persons best demonstrate their sense of relatedness, responsibility and stewardship.

4

The Developmental Side of the Stewardship Pattern

Society depends for its existence on the inviolable personal solitude of its members. Society, to merit its name, must be made up not of numbers, or of mechanical units, but of persons. To be a person implies responsibility and freedom, and both these imply a certain interior solitude, a sense of personal integrity, a sense of one's own reality and of one's ability to give himself to society. [Thomas Merton][1]

Being socially transcendent does not necessarily mean living in isolation. As we have seen, people experience social transcendence regardless of economics, social circumstances or living arrangements. Their detachment or objectivity becomes activated the moment they are aware of having a distinct self, a self whose reality is separate from the society in which they live.

This detachment ultimately provides them with the distance needed for their ongoing communion with the higher self—a communion which then stimulates and supports their personality growth. As the individual's whole-seeing and whole-thinking develop—as he begins to separate from his own "little" perceptions, ego-interests and preoccupations—he is able to open up into a relationship with others, a relationship based on a life which is becoming more authentic. In fact, it is

only through the vitality and trustworthiness of the authenti-
cally-lived life that relatedness to others can be sustained. Such
relatedness requires strength, the ability to overlook the foibles
and foolishness of others and the patience and maturity to be
able to give to others without becoming emotionally scattered
or swept away by the instabilities, pressures or manipulations
of the outside world.

As people discover their own realities, they are also more
able to give the gift of themselves, because there is a real self
to give. In concert, the study participants expressed the desire
to give of themselves, a desire grounded in a perspective that
sees the other-as-self. They demonstrated an increased ability
to act in ways that contribute to the well-being, care and needs
of others. I call this tendency the stewardship pattern.

In the original Judeo-Christian tradition, the word *stewardship* meant servanthood: the care and management of God's
resources, both material and human. This idea had its begin-
nings in the earliest chapters of the Old Testament, where man
had no existence apart from God; where Abba, Yahweh and
God were all words used to describe the supreme Father to
whom all were responsible, apart from whom no one had any
life at all, and who, from the beginning of time, created man
to care for the earth. Genesis 2:15 teaches us, "The Lord God
took the man and put him in the Garden of Eden to till and
keep it." Not only is man created to take care of the garden,
but he is also expected to nurture and protect all human life in
it.

Judging from the many times man is counseled and rep-
rimanded on this issue, he may not have been prepared to carry
out God's high expectations. While equality and justice are special themes throughout both the Old and the New Testaments,
it is in the Old Testament that we read of God dealing most
harshly with those who forget their obligations to behave responsibly toward others. God takes an active interest in how

man treats his fellow man and how he manages his life and affairs in general. God regularly intervenes to punish those who misbehave or who are callous toward others. He takes personal interest in all who are his, freeing the oppressed in order to help them through their trials and sufferings, and condemning and punishing the rich whenever they mistreat or forget to give to the poor. God's clear and continual message to man in this early stage of his time on earth is that socially responsible behavior is the expected standard.[2] "The earth is the Lord's and all the fullness thereof," Psalm 24:1 instructs—man is supposed to take an active, responsible caretaker's role if he desires to fulfill God's plan.

Thus, the original premise of stewardship had a threefold root: that there is a responsible servant in the form of each and every human, that there is a definite entrustment to the servant of everything that belongs to God, and that there is an ultimate accounting to God for the way the earth and all its people are cared for.

Within this traditional perspective, man not only glorifies God as he makes good and prudent use of whatever he has been given to manage, but he also honors God's expectations for him as he serves others and treats them as his brothers and sisters. Moreover, man is severely punished when he fails to act as a good steward.

Because the Bible can be read and interpreted on many levels, the early concept of stewardship could be understood through a developmental, psychological model as well as a religious one. Viewing the stewardship concept developmentally, we might come to understand God—as described in the Old Testament—as a stern ever-watchful parent who knows that his young, immature children need a lot of training in self-control before they can internalize the idea of relating properly to others and to things.

The immature, underdeveloped personality *is* impulsive,

opportunistic and self-involved. In the mature human, greed and self-obsession have given way to generosity, selflessness, and a disciplined will that *can* give to others. When we speak of "arrested development" in people, we mean adults whose grown-up bodies actually are housing children. These are persons who, despite advanced chronological age, see narrowly, perhaps in an infantile way, are emotionally blocked or rebellious, and are fixated—stuck—when they encounter obstacles or problems in life. Some experience that should have been dealt with and assimilated was repressed into the unconscious realm of the personality, leaving the individual neurotic because he is still responding to life, and trying to solve his daily problems, out of the framework of infantile perceptions.

For the immature personality, fear is often a prime motivator for right action. Rules, laws, restrictions and the threat of punishment for forbidden actions are all ways to insure that the individual controls himself. A childish mentality does not love self-control, so it requires external control for its safety and well-being, and for the safety and well-being of others. For example, a youngster needs strict guidelines and forceful consequences to learn to leave matches alone or to remember to look both ways before crossing the street. In like fashion, mankind in its childhood probably needed authoritarian guidance, even occasional slaps on the hand, to learn to behave itself.

It is only later in man's development that a novel element—that of love—is introduced. We first read of love, *agape*, in the New Testament through the radical teachings of Jesus Christ. This new perspective and call, which continues to impact the stewardship principle today, no doubt emerged only when mankind was ready—even if only to a slight degree—to hear what Jesus had to teach. His actions, expectations and life teach us what it means to love one another from a generous, mature spirit. He shows us how to express mature love. He demonstrates to us—through every word and deed—

how to minister to others, how to care for them, and how to make choices from our highest, most responsible self.

These are not easy lessons for anyone to learn; the earliest Christians also apparently needed lots of repetition. The Pauline epistles contain frequent lectures in which Paul and other disciples try to get their followers to grow up. "But I, brethren, could not address you as spiritual men, but as men of the flesh, as babes in Christ. I fed you with milk, not solid food; for you were not ready for it; and even yet you are not ready, for you are still of the flesh. For while there is jealousy and strife among you, are you not . . . behaving like ordinary men?" (1 Cor 3:1–4). Again in Hebrews 5:12–14, Paul continues to scold his people in frustrated tones, saying, "For though by this time you ought to be teachers, you need some one to teach you again the first principles of God's word. You need milk, not solid food; for every one who lives on milk is unskilled in the word of righteousness, for he is a child. But solid food is for the mature. . . ."

Paul is rightly concerned that the deeper aspects of faith, of God, of man's intimate relationship to God cannot be absorbed or properly handled by someone who is still a child in his understanding and emotions.

From a developmental frame of reference, it is certain that Jesus of Nazareth was a whole, self-realized, and completed personality—the epitome of the enlightened man. His active, continual and eternal demonstration of love exemplifies what human love could be, were we developed and mature ourselves. Love, dependability, empathic understanding, a generous spirit, the ability to experience another as oneself, keeping one's word, the ability to affirm life fully in the face of death—these are all traits which flow from a supremely well-defined and developed consciousness, from a will which gives the self-mastery to say, "Thy will be done," and from the commitment which gives the wherewithal to follow through, regardless of sacrifices or discomfort. While Cain asks "Am I my brother's keeper?" the New Man responds by selflessly giving his life for his brothers.

Christ's lessons of brotherly love and personal responsibility are very different from what was taught in the Old Testament. The New Testament calls mankind to a higher level of functioning, a higher faculty of consciousness. It teaches us to love ourselves and *all* others from an inner awareness and trust of love. We are told that this kind of love, consciously enacted, transcends self-concern and has little to do with fear of punishment. Rather, it is a by-product of our development, our self-discipline, our newly-found personal power—a power born of an intimate relationship with God. Thus, Jesus advocated abandoning fear and boldly choosing to act from a deep sense of trust, of union with the Father, and a sense of interrelationship with others.

His life and teachings, and those of his disciples, remain a radical call for personal and social transformation. It is a radical call because it isn't automatic. The teachings of the New Testament run counter to our all-too-natural tendency to be self-serving; to focus narrowly on our own interest, family or community perspective: our desire to compromise our selfhood by adjusting to the norms of society; our reluctance to develop those high faculties within ourselves which would enable us to be a potential instrument or servant of God. In other words, the New Testament asks that we become fully human, that we serve from love instead of from fear or a sense of obligation, that we demonstrate a type of love which asks for everything we have. It is in this kind of maturity, in this kind of personal development, that true stewardship is rooted.

Contemporary American society offers many examples of stewardship in action through its social and environmental programs. These appear to be growing. The environmentalist movement stresses the needs of the future as it seeks to protect, respect and preserve wildlife, the wilderness and our earth's resources. The increasing network of national and international agencies, both secular and religiously-based, which have sprung up to house, feed and protect the rights of the poor and those living in the streets is another stewardly movement. The massive national attention and community support now given to battered women and children, the elderly and the handicapped is still another example of how citizens are collectively demonstrating their care for and feelings of relatedness to others. These programs, however political they may appear and however slick their marketing campaigns may be, are at the individual level of giving signs that the idea of stewardship—the idea of caring for others—exists in our nation's collective consciousness.

For an individual, stewardship is expressed as a potent giving of self. It is egoless in that, through giving, the mature individual serves higher needs than his own comfort, safety and gratification. He gives because he directly experiences another's needs and concerns as his own—not because of external pressures or fear of retribution or the desire to impress others with his generosity and piousness.

Of course, individuals give in differing ways and degrees, both of their material possessions and of themselves. But for the mature person, gifts of the self always flow out of generosity and unselfishness, out of the emotion of love, *agape*—concern for the other. As we will see in the next chapter, it is this spirit of giving that transforms duty into pleasure, and livelihood into calling.

5

Gifts of Self As Stewardship

As each has received a gift, employ it for one another, as good stewards of God's varied grace. [Peter 4:10]

Gifts of the self are so varied that there is no easy way to list or categorize them. They include giving time to others or getting involved with their problems—even the projected concerns of future generations, such as the stewardly acts of the environmentalists or medical research. A gift of self might be one's application of energy and effort to a vocation in a way which then allows natural talents and aptitudes to be shared with others. One's gift might be the development of patience or learning to live in harmony with others, with nature or with the demands of an occupation, organization or career. There are gifts of time, money or one's own personality so that the strengths within the deepest part of the psyche become a source of inspiration or support to others.

Whatever the form, the potency and force of love is always present to some degree in true giving. As we have seen, love is dependent on the relative presence of maturity, empathy and an evolved *self* which has something to give.

In giving the gift of the self, the individual gives from *strength*—not from a weakened, fearful or exploitive self which gives out of submission to external pressures or which seeks to get something from another through the act of his giving.

Because each has a distinctiveness, as he develops his specific talents and skills, he will have much to offer from the wellspring of the real self. To talk about giving from any other perspective is to relegate the act to a mechanistic human response, a response generated by any number of negative motives or culturally-induced and unconscious habits.

In the attitudes and actions of the people in this study we find a threefold psychology of stewardship. The *first* aspect of this pattern is that the giver desires a deeper, fuller identity with his own gifts. He wants to discover his unique talents and then use these in a way that offers something of value to others. In other words, productiveness is tied to genuine giving which, in turn, is linked to self-knowledge.

The *second* characteristic of stewardship is that the giver experiences a kinship, or sense of relatedness, to others. This quality is significant because, as we have seen, it is impossible to genuinely care for others, to be considerate of the earth and all its life forms, without a real sense of involvement with others.

Paradoxically, the socially-transcendent person who at first steps outside the bounds of ordinary living is uniquely qualified to be a steward. It is this individual who ultimately overcomes the feelings of separation, fear and anxiety which are symptoms of powerlessness and an underdeveloped character structure. It is the actualizing, whole individual who achieves a sense of union with others.

Third, the good steward, as he develops, progressively expresses a potent, dynamic type of love—a love which *is* giving and which the individual exhibits through his thoughts, works and social activities.

This chapter examines each of these qualities of stewardship in more detail and also provides an illustration of how these traits are acted out by the study participants.

The first quality of stewardship is a desire to discover,

then express, one's own unique gifts and to use these to benefit self-and-other. Study participants viewed work as an integral part of life, not as something split into a duality of working vs. personal life. They see work as an activity that emanates from the innermost self, as a mirror of the self. Whether people worked in solitude—as writers, researchers or artists—or as educators or business persons, they viewed their work as a natural, spontaneous and seemingly effortless extension of themselves. In this way, personal gifts were translated into fruits others could enjoy.

The magical artist Ben Shahn once said that every artist who expresses the depth and subjective truths of his life gives something of value and wonder to others. In the same way, as the socially transcendent individual develops a better understanding of what exists within him that is unique, distinctive and of value, as he is able to express that self in the outer forms of working or personal life, he gives something to others which is original and truthful. Consequently, his gifts retain a vitality, force and freshness which distinguish them from the set of mundane outcomes usually experienced from work.

For most people, work is only a means to an end—money, power, recognition, status. Work is not loved for itself—as an expression of the self. However, almost all study participants described their work as important to them, as easy, like play. That is not to say that they viewed their work as frivolous, or that they came to it without a responsible attitude, or that it didn't require effort. Work was something they *preferred* to do almost above all else. They didn't need or desire recreational activities in order to feel good, to relax or escape job pressures. There was no evidence that participants were using work to stave off feelings of anxiety in order to distance themselves from others. Neither was there any comment about outdoing another through the work vehicle, or using work to gain status in the eyes of others. Even material gain took a back seat to the individual's interest and personal involvement with the tasks and ideas of his work.

For example, a teacher said she felt her work affected eternity and that she worked for the "joy of seeing kids learn. I teach in the trust that there is a future for humanity. My work is play. It is self-expression. It gives meaning, structure and purpose to my whole life."

A city manager described his work as "helping me fulfill my destiny. Whether I'm helping the local public school design curriculum for environmental education, or participating in a civic organization, or out in the field supervising one of the clean-up projects, it makes no difference to me. It's all a way to do what I do best within the context of what others may call 'work.' "

A potter described his work as a "way of seeing." For him, work was a teacher and a mirror. "My working process often dictates to me what to do next (in life). I have little need for material possessions: the only things I have left are my tools and my car. The answer to all my problems is just to make another pot."

A poet said, "All my time is leisure time, even when I do what is termed 'work.' This is because my work is play. All play/work is important to me, and I take it seriously. Every word is me expressing myself. That can be frightening when I'm off-center and fine when I'm on-center. Anyway I look at it, it's always me in the work."

A carpenter described his working life as less important in terms of what he did than *how* he did it. "I'm very concerned about how I do a job or project, more so than what I do," he said. "The how gives me satisfaction or the impetus to improve myself, and tells me about myself each step of the way. But I don't really feel I have a job or work that's different from the way I am in every part of my life. I am what I do, if you know what I mean—it's basically the same."

These comments help us understand the cohesive self/
world/other view of life which develops in the actualizing person. From a motivational perspective, these persons are
"metamotivated," to use Abraham Maslow's phrase. In other
words, they are no longer concerned about filling basic needs,
such as security, survival or status. Their actions are stirred
from within, from the innermost spontaneous core of themselves to express that which they personally experience as real,
beautiful and true.

In describing the actualized person's attitude toward
work, Maslow writes:

> . . . in all cases, at least in our culture, they are dedicated
> people, devoted to some task "outside themselves," some
> vocation, or duty, or beloved job. Generally the devotion
> and dedication is so marked that one can fairly use the old
> words vocation, calling or mission to describe their pas-
> sionate, selfless and profound feeling for their "work." We
> could even use the words destiny or fate. I have sometimes
> gone so far as to speak of oblation in the religious sense, in
> the sense of offering oneself or dedicating oneself upon
> some altar for some particular task, some cause outside
> oneself and bigger than oneself, something not merely self-
> ish, something impersonal.[1]

This attitude toward work naturally leads to the second
quality of stewardship: the feeling of relatedness to others.
Some study participants, sounding much like citizens of the
Old Testament, said that they felt a "duty" toward others. As
one woman put it, "I'd say we have an obligation to help the
poor, the hungry, those in prison. In short, we have a duty to
take care of others."

Most were more joyful about the whole matter of giving,
expressing their sense of oneness with others as a richly felt fusion with all of life, a unity experienced as something sacred.

As later chapters will reveal, these feelings are probable signs that the individual has at least a bit of the mystic sense, experiencing himself as part of an intricate and infinite web of creation.

Said one study subject, "I feel we're all divine, are all linked mysteriously, while each of us remains separate, unique, even mundane. This separate/unique and related/linked paradox means we need to respect, even encourage, the diversity amongst ourselves, maintaining a clear core of self all the while and serving each other, too." Someone else wrote, "I feel myself to be pretty much like others in that our basic needs are the same and, bottom line, we all want the same things: a place in the sun, respect, the ability to take care of ourselves and our own, and the hope that we'll live forever, surrounded by those we love and need."

People perceive their relatedness to others and to the world only as they develop, only as they internalize the ethical, integrated characteristics of maturity and enlightenment. Of course, there are degrees of maturity and enlightenment. But as relatedness is lived through all the various aspects of life, the individual comes to view himself as integrated with others. Without this perception, personality wholeness cannot exist, because others will always have characteristics we haven't accepted in ourselves.

Eventually the feeling that the other is very much like us eliminates the sense of separation and isolation, allowing the individual to bond to others as well as to the deepest parts of himself. The growing sense that one is a part of everyone else can be expressed in many ways: as a poignant caring for other, as feelings that the other's joy and pain is much like one's own, or even as self-acceptance, since by accepting our shortcomings we more humbly take our place among other human beings.

Whatever words they used to describe their sense of relatedness, all study participants exhibited some perception of connectedness. This is evident both from what they *say* they feel, and from what they *do* to serve others in their communities.

One woman said, "I seem to care intensely about those who are victims of injustice. Sometimes now I feel a growing unity, a responsibility and an obligation to people in general." Another, a retired woman, talked about her community stewardship in this way: "My work is now gardening, canning, 'baby' sitting, tutoring, playing the piano in a nearby nursing home, visiting prisoners, and looking for other ways to 'work' with and serve others. I hope to get better, be better as a person, as I get older—I'll be sixty-three next month. I believe in mutual support. My husband and I cooperate with neighbors to a significant degree. We're even living in a fledgling community where cooperation, in terms of growing food collectively and exchanging needed services, is the expected standard. And a satisfying thing it is at that."

Another retired woman described how her sense of relatedness governed her life choices and activities. Although she worked as an accountant throughout her professional life, she had originally wanted to enter some sort of Christian service. For various reasons, that goal didn't materialize, so she used her business and accounting skills to earn a livelihood and then devoted herself to community service projects and church work in her off-work hours. She said, "I've known since I was eighteen that I wanted to do some kind of service work. I was fortunate in that I worked at an easy job, and had energy and time after hours to work with people. I've looked for ways to serve others, to fill a need that might exist. I feel much happier when I'm doing that. Now that I'm retired, I can give all my time to service and church-related projects. I teach creative writing to an adult group, I teach reading to another group through the Literary Volunteers of America, and I've always been active—even at the national level—in my church.

"I recall back when I was a youngster, in church they'd pass around collection barrels to gather tithes and offerings. The slogan on those barrels was, 'Others first.' That slogan has stuck with me all these years.

"I'm seventy-three now, and have learned that when I put my mind on others, it helps me get my mind off myself, not in a way that puts me down, but in a way that lets me forget myself, even helps me feel happier. I don't give of myself because I 'should'—I don't like the word 'should' because that makes me feel I have to do something, and takes the joy out of it for me. I'm just selfishly doing what makes me happy."

Other study participants expressed how they acted on their feelings of connectedness through their work. "If you've read *Goodbye Mr. Chips* then you know how I feel about my work," said a teacher. "For me teaching is a way of developing a family—not in the personalized way most people think of, but as Mr. Chips said in the final pages of the book. When someone said to him that it was too bad he didn't have children of his own, he answered, 'It's wrong to think I've had no children. I've had hundreds and hundreds of children.' And that's exactly how I feel. I believe I'm doing a service for lots and lots of people. The things I do, whether it be teaching or involving myself in my church, have a sort of social mysticism for me. It's the way I engage in the world, but at the same time I experience God in myself and in others. These things I do are truly how I bring God into being."

An environmentalist told how feelings of connectedness affected his approach to his work. "I have a reverence for nature, a humility regarding past generations and people, a desire to honor some of the traditions of the past and those who have come before me. Being raised in a Sunday school, Christian environment must have influenced me as I was growing up. I recall a sense of outrage when I heard of social injustices and saw them happening to people. I guess I could call my desire to be concerned, my need to translate this concern into practical outcomes, a 'calling.' If I were to describe the personal attributes that have helped me be happy and productive, I'd say my caring for others lets me be happy. This feeling is grounded in an optimism and what I can only call a gentleness for all life. Caring for others and the environment fills me with happiness."

Another man, a carpenter and naturalist, described his perceptions of his life and work in this way: "Living *is* meaning. It's probably through my work that I express love. These days I experience a lot of love just being part of this lovely forest. For example, there's a bird here called a night hawk. It comes by every year around this time, is very endearing, and has become a regular visitor here. If I had to identify what it would mean to be my highest self, I'd say it would be learning to live as softly as possible, without making a big footprint on the earth."

The common thread through all the above statements seems to me to be the sense of unity each person feels with other people and the world. These individuals speak from a world-view that feels no real separation and which sees no true strangers. This is not to say that the individual feels the same as everyone he meets, believing he must conform to the wishes and standards of others, or relate completely with the values of others. Rather, to the extent that he is most truly himself, he experiences a link with others and with the natural world. The unitive sense means oneness—not sameness. It is the foundational attitude for the giving of self.

Finally, the third quality of stewardship—the giving of self through a strong emotion of love—flows spontaneously out of the interrelated world view. As we have seen, some study participants expressed their giving as "duty," but hadn't yet reached that level of development where they actively *desired* to give; their stewardship seemed to be more an intellectual, "head" matter rather than a heart concern.

For those in the study who are more highly actualized, serving others is an essential part of life, almost something which the individual has no choice about. To these persons, work and leisure are integrated activities. Thus, all one's life is perceived as service. The total personality dedicates itself to giving, even for those working in isolation, such as writers, artists and scientists. *Not* to give would be experienced as deprivation, as some missing ingredient in life.

Those who spoke of their work in strongly vocational, devotional terms exemplify the highly actualized individual's way of giving through his talents. These people *become* their work; they sacrifice everything to it, not in such a way that their efforts are strained, pressure-ridden or unbalanced, but rather in a manner that creates a fully-functioning, effective personality, one that is totally absorbed by the work. The potency of such a working life becomes obvious. These personalities teach us about the power and force of love, since that is what their giving truly is.

In his now-classic book, *The Art of Loving,* Erich Fromm reminds us that love involves activity, not passivity, that it is a giving of self rather than a receiving from another, and that this type of giving strengthens the individual rather than diminishing him.

"Love is an activity," Fromm writes, "not a passive affect; it is a 'standing in,' not a falling for . . . the active character of love can be described by stating that love is primarily giving, not receiving . . . [and] for the productive character, giving is the highest expression of potency. In the very act of giving I experience my strength, my wealth, my power. . . . Giving is more joyous than receiving because in the act of giving lies the expression of my aliveness."[2]

The statement of a young environmentalist in the study serves as an excellent illustration of just this kind of aliveness.

Living on less than five thousand dollars per year, he describes his life this way:

"I'd say the quality of my life is rich. That's the way I feel when I wake up in the morning. My little house is small, and I live without electricity, without many of the amenities people call 'modern.' But when I look around me, I see that everything is luscious: I live in a beautiful house, I'm surrounded by forests, sunlight and gorgeous, opulent trees. Culturally, I'm surrounded by people who care for me, and whom I care about. Politically and religiously there's every type of activity I could wish for. I get lots of hugs, affection, approval and kindnesses of all types from the people in my community. I feel rich. There's no other way to describe it."

Although he isn't specifically talking about work, his vibrancy and perceptual sense of abundance and beauty stems, at least in part, from his total involvement with his work. It has special meaning for him; he describes it as a "calling."

His sentiments do not much differ from those of Thomas Merton as he reflects upon the richness of his own life, even though he lives in a way others might call poor.

Merton wrote, "I cannot say I am making much money. I get $45 per month, plus room and board. Yet, the life I lead here is as happy as the richest kind of life and, as far as I am concerned, just as comfortable. How can I write about poverty when, though I am in a way poor, yet I still live as though in a country club?"[3]

This consciousness of abundance is a characteristic of the actualized person, who experiences love as his ground of being. He has attained a deep awareness of the infinite richness, intricacy and order of the universe (as we will see in a later chapter on the peak experience)—an awareness which itself is a sign of the illumined personality. To a great extent, such a consciousness is "goal-less," feels as if it *has* everything, and is motivated to give from the experience of having attained everything it needs. Because the actualized personality has experienced itself as "completed" (i.e., needing nothing, not having deficits, etc.), it *sees* the world richly, *even when* its five senses contradict such opulence.

Later in our interview, the environmentalist quoted above said that what makes him happy is to give of himself:

"I'm highly involved in this community through my work, and in fact sometimes I get spread too thin and then have to cut back. I will say I experience every activity as fulfilling: I write, I have a radio program which is basically my way of educating large numbers of people. I'm involved in political action in such a manner that I feel I'm accomplishing something of real value. I'm living out the things that mean a great deal to me in my community, and in very practical ways at that. I feel so fortunate to be in a position to give of myself in these ways, and the fact that others are willing to receive what I'm giving is a thrill."

A painter described his work in much the same way. Through his sentiments we can feel the vigor, potency and total commitment which he puts into his art:

"My work is not recreational. It requires commitment of a sort I find hard to express. I never thought of it until now, but I live for the work. This must be what it's like to be a politician—you do it twenty-four hours a day. It's more than work. It's preoccupation with the ideas of your occupation. I live for the work, and I am the work. My work seems to be my life. I don't really *go* to work, since I live what I do."

A peace activist helps us understand the similarities between these working attitudes and a religious vocation, even though earlier in our conversation she rejected any notion of having religious feelings herself. "I'm not spiritual," she said of herself. "I'm earthy, perhaps soulful, but I hate all that empty form-without-content which I saw in organized reli-

gions and which I felt when my family and I went to church
. . . so I wouldn't say I am religious or even spiritual now."
Later in our interview she described her work in this way:
"I live my life with a full consciousness of others, including nature, rather than coming from a 'me first' point of view.
Of course, this attitude is part of everything I do: my work, the
way I live, the way I relate to people. I'd say my work is a calling. I can't *not* do it. The most important thing I feel I can do
right now is educate people to the dangers of nuclear war. This
sense, or calling, has grown steadily over the past two and a half
years. I feel everything else I do is secondary to this goal. It's
as if I've had a conversion experience and have been taken over
by these feelings; in a real way I've been taken over by my desire to share these ideas and convictions with others."

The entire motivational thrust of the stewardship pattern,
as described here, is a generous one since it originates from the
positive, pleasureful and highly charged impulses of the actualizing personality.

Such personalities go about their giving in what might appear to be selfish ways. They exclude many conventional activities—perhaps even certain people—from their lives. They
are people who have discovered what, for them, has meaning
and truth and they have taken steps to bring that to fruition in
their daily actions and choices. In varying degrees, such persons show us the paradox of wholeness: as each dedicates himself unwaveringly to a self-affirming life (and *this* is what others
often will label as "selfish") a power and an increased ability
to love is born.

It is a love which empowers the individual to be self-affirming. This emotion also fuels his intuitive leap of faith *inward*. Ultimately, his inward leap is what sparks the strength
and will to selflessly give to others. The pacifist in our study
describes how concentration, discipline and purposefulness increase as personality wholeness is cultivated:

"I don't indulge myself as I used to. I now control my social life so as not to get involved in things that distracted me from my work but which are not very interesting or purposeful for me. I'm so focused now, much more than most people I know. . . . What I want to do more than anything else—more than I thought I could want anything—is to educate people to the dangers of nuclear war, and in that way help build a safe and peaceful place for all of us to live."

The actualized personality develops along the lines of his strengths. For the mystic—an elevated, spiritual and distinct personality—these strengths are decidely religious, as is his development.

Our next chapter describes the way in which the mystic interprets all of life, including his work, as having its source in God. For the mystic, living, working and relating to others all occur within the context of God-consciousness. Meister Eckhardt, a perfected mystic, exemplifies this consciousness with these words:

> The wood does not change the fire into itself, but the fire changes the wood into itself. So are we changed into God, that we shall know him as he is.[4]

And so it is that in our next chapters we describe how the mystic becomes more and more filled with the awareness of God.

Part Two:

The Way of The Mystic

Cheap grace is the grace we bestow on ourselves. . . . Costly grace is the treasure hidden in the
field; for the sake of it a man will gladly go and sell
all that he has. It is the pearl of great price to buy
which the merchant will sell all his goods. . . .
Costly grace is the gospel which must be sought
again and again, the gift which must be asked for,
the door at which a man must knock. Such grace is
costly because it calls us to follow. . . . It is costly
because it costs a man his life, and it is grace because
it gives a man the only true life. [Dietrich Bonhoeffer, *The Cost of Discipleship*]

6

The Mystic Type Along The Way

What human beings through all centuries and throughout the world are really good at is defending themselves against the love of God. [Study Participant, Alabama]

Only in mystics do we observe the full expanse of mankind's spiritual potential. For the mystic, daily life and moment-to-moment thought are linked intimately with spiritual issues. The mystic taps into and cultivates the deepest levels of his intuitive and subjective self—so much so that writers such as Evelyn Underhill and Richard Bucke, long-time researchers of the mystic type, suggested that the mystic develops new and extended faculties of perception—abilities which lift him "above" other people, perhaps even marking a species within our species. What sets the mystic apart is that he is "in love with the Absolute," to use Underhill's phrase.

Mystics are a definite type of person. They have a distinctive life's course, and their mission—regardless of their country or culture of origin—is always the same: to find their way "back" to that Absolute Reality which they sense is the One True Reality, and from which they believe they've come.

A key difference between mystics and all others is that their spiritual eyes have been opened, and they have "seen." From the chaos of their early inner confusion, mystics awaken to an illumined posture of Being. They are in a state of Being,

75

rather than—like most others—seeking to become. Mystics are our poets and artists, our intuitional, creative thinkers, our inventors and saints.

They possess such a high degree of interior richness that with little effort—or so it may seem to others—they develop their latent powers of transcending ordinary reality.

One study participant commented about some of the ways he transcends normal reality: "Last Sunday, [in church] I tried a new way of centering down, and was prompted to try Eckhart's way. . . . Graphically, this could be called putting oneself in God's shoes and 'knowing' from this perspective. As I felt my way into this, there was speaking within me—like within the Old Testament prophets—the voice of God, using human words. . . . What was remarkable about this was the heightened sense of needs which I perceived. I 'knew' everyone, including myself, very much more clearly and intuitively than before. I 'knew' with a sort of detachment which let me focus on the needs of others without getting messed up with my own emotional responses. This clear seeing, which I'd rather not call clairvoyance, seemed to go beyond my previous perceptions of people. I have since rather easily been able to return to this without finding the speaking forced, stilted or artificial. Romans 8:26 may point to this mode of prayer; otherwise, I have never encountered it in reading before."

Because the mystic himself is involved in a life-changing process, transmutating his ordinary self into his higher Self, the *way* of the mystic—which is to say, his life's journey—and his personal psychology are merged.

The mystic's experience gave birth to the whole sphere of transpersonal psychology, which has been described as differing from ordinary therapies (e.g., Freudian, Adlerian, etc.) in one critical way: while the latter help people cope with their fears, nightmares and passions, transpersonal psychology, on the other hand, helps them *awaken*. If the mystic's ability to see and hear the things of God—i.e., of a Transcendent reality—can be trusted (and I believe it can), then we might say that the mystic represents the one who is awake, or—at the very least—is in the process of awakening.

Very few of the people in this study consider themselves true mystics. However, my hunch is that some of the study participants are approaching a state of illumination, a state of being. I have therefore included comments by only those few participants who readily identify with the mystic's profile (who, for example, recall their transcendent experiences, are willing to describe their spiritual or mystical experiences, etc.) throughout the rest of this chapter. In this way I hope to underscore for the reader the principles of the psychology of mysticism by illustrating the points with the words and sentiments of those who wholeheartedly embrace the mystic position.

Underhill cites three elements which characterize the mystic way. I am indebted to her research in that it serves as a foundation for my own. She states:

1. Mysticism is a transformative approach to life rather than a theoretical "playing" with ideas.
2. Mysticism involves spiritual activity, representing the individual's absorption and deepening relationship with God. This activity absolutely influences and dominates the mystic's path and is inseparable from it. Thus the mystic and his "path" are one.
3. The mystic's dominant life-emotion becomes love. This emotional state shows itself in his progressively strengthened dedication of will toward the things of God: the expression of his will in daily life; service to him through work, relationships and everyday choices; and sacrifices of the physical/mental body in order to experience him, pay honor to him. Although the mystic may not "appear" to be an active participant in the world (i.e., he may be more con-

templative and non-doing—in the Taoistic sense—than most people), in fact his entire world-view is dedicated to God, and—as Thomas Merton often wrote—his life's work is *being*, is life itself, and is not specifically one profession or another.

First, in terms of the practical, transformative nature of the mystic's life, we might compare it to a rebirthing process, which usually starts with a conversion experience. We will examine the conversion experience in our next chapter. Suffice it to say at this time that the mystic process ends (although certainly not in a life-terminating way) with the individual's complete experiential (as opposed to merely intellectual) union with God. This rebirth can take a lifetime to manifest itself or it can happen in an instant, as apparently it did with Saint Paul, who in typical mystic's phraseology said, "To live is Christ, and to die is gain." His sentiment is permeated with that rhapsodic ardor which characterizes the mystic's rebirth. For once the rebirth process has taken hold, the individual is never his own again, and—by a complete renewal of mind and heart—lives his life in the Absolute, his entire personality being taken over by a consciousness of the Transcendent.

The mystic longs to know the Ultimate Reality as his own—both by direct experience and by personal relationship. One individual in the study, for example, a carpenter living in total solitude in California's coastal redwood forest, described his longing for God in this way: "The one constant in my life, the one integrative desire, is my longing to connect with the unity of the universe. I guess you'd call that God. This is the one thing of value in my life, the thing that keeps me going."

Another man, also living in solitude, wrote me a follow-up letter after our inperson interview in which he described his "thirst for transformation" with these words: "I consider my involvement in [this project] one of the active concerns in my life because it directly mirrors the transformation I have been going through, am going through . . . and desire to 'complete.' "

Another participant said, "I see an importance in the moment—this moment—this point when everything is ending and all is beginning. I try to touch this as often as possible."

Underhill's research indicates that there are two distinct thrusts or directions to the full mystic consciousness. One is the increasing vision or consciousness of God; the other is the inner transmutation of the personality, the rebuilding or restructuring of the self on an inward and deeply, all pervasive level. Neither thrust can be accomplished, as we shall see, without the complete transcendence of the small, egocentric self.

"The end and object of this 'inward alchemy' will be the raising of the whole self to the condition in which conscious and permanent union with the Absolute takes place; and man, ascending to the summit of his manhood, enters into that greater life for which he was made."[1]

The true mystic is not merely involved with esoteric thoughts or beautiful images of God and heaven. He is totally absorbed in a life-movement, a journey in which his essential self—his real self—comes into life with and *in* God. This "coming to God," as it has been called, *is* the journey. Its goal is to live in such a way that there is no distinction between daily activity (i.e., one's business, chores—like washing dishes or scrubbing floors—walking in the streets, shopping, etc.) and prayer, worship or remembrance of God. In other words, the true mystic desires that his life be subsumed in, and with, the presence of God.

There are stages along the mystic way—stages which have been interpreted differently by various writers, but which fall into several distinct *levels* of personal growth. The intuitional step is first. This can best be described as an inner prompting, perhaps a sudden moment of insight, when the individual senses that there is more to life than his ordinary living currently reveals. This awakening can come either in a core-religious experience (also called a conversion experience, a moment of illumination, or a peak-experience during which the individual's mind becomes silent, still or "vanishes") or as an ongoing, increasing "knowing" that the Absolute reality is the one (and *only*) true and worthwhile life.

However it starts, the mystic's journey involves a subsequent pulling-away from the world: a distancing, emotional detachment, a way of life that is contemplative and simplified (which may parallel what in mystic terminology is called "purification")—that life-posture designed to unite the individual most completely with the Transcendent nature of reality by removing him from the pulls and enticements of the world[2] and, ultimately, fusion with God.

These stages follow the configuration of social transcendence which I have described in earlier chapters. We have seen how an individual's separation and social detachment can eventually lead to growth. The mystic's path also involves initial detachment, and like the secular monk, the mystic reassesses old images, cultural beliefs and past programing. He too must assimilate and integrate new perceptions, values and emotions into his life.

However, whereas the monk may seek his answers in social solutions, the mystic *always* organizes his life through the religious solution—finding personal answers in the Transcendent. When he does act in the social sphere, his motivating drive is always to pay homage to the Truth, to God, to that silent, "small still voice" within. After all, the term self-transcendence means that the former personality is dissolved, that the lesser, the culturally defined self—with its idealized images and constricting socially-produced outer shell—collapses, giving way to the larger, the real Self.

I would guess, and only further research could confirm, that the mystic's journey is a natural extension of inner work that already has begun in the socially transcendent person. But the inner transformation which takes place in the mystic extends beyond that of the secular monk in that he *seeks* to live his life in a complete and intimate relationship with God. The secular monk—however detached and stewardly he may be in his life's efforts—does not always express himself in spiritual terms. The mystic always does. "The mystic," wrote Underhill, ". . . dwells in a world unknown to other men. He pierces the veil of imperfection, and beholds Creation with the Creator's eye."[3]

A study participant wrote of her own "awakened spirit" in this way: "I feel as though I'm walking with God all the time now. Little, insignificant things happen to me that make me feel his presence. I feel he's a part of me and that I'm a part of him. There is a sort of inner light in and around me, although I know it's not a visible thing, and I don't actually visualize it. The point of all of this is that I've gained the strength to live a more potent life, a genuine and authentic life, a life of kindness. Some of my friends wanted me to go with them on a trip to the Holy Land, with our church—you know, to be nearer to God. But I told them, 'No.' I don't have to walk in the Holy Land or travel to some other part of the world to know God. He's with me all the time and everywhere."

The mystic's life-altering path always results in a radical dropping away of the former self and a restructuring of that self in the apprehension of God. Gradually or suddenly, the mystic relates differently to others, abandoning social and material interests in the world in favor of another realm—the supernatural or transcendent world. This life-movement makes physical, social and personal sacrifices possible, even mandatory. These would be experienced by anyone but the mystic as major psychic-surgery—such is the currency, urgency and intensity of the sacrifices called for. They might range from seemingly minor ego-bruising choices to the complete surrender of key comforts, securities or even life itself as in the contemporary example of Gandhi, who time and again put himself into political and personal danger as a way of expressing Truth.

The mystic defines his sacrifices as being necessary to fulfill a higher Truth of life. One study participant, describing a difficult personal choice, put it this way: "I notice that fear is leaving me, although not entirely. However, I see myself acting more than before in certain risk-taking ways, and doing so with the backdrop of feeling that the death of my body has nothing to do with me. Jesus said that we shouldn't fear the one who would harm our body, and that's becoming clearer to me.

"For example, I'm planning to refuse to pay some taxes under the War Refusal Tax category. There is fear in me, since I live in an area where there's not much support for that kind of thing. This fear, however, is balanced by a certainty of consciousness that this is what I must do. . . . The act represents the way in which I believe the teachings of Christ would have us go."

The costs of the mystic's journey are made even greater by the fact that this is a private transition, almost impossible to communicate to others. Again, the transition necessitates self-transcendence: that lifting out, up and away from the socialized, encultured personality as it has been understood by the individual (and his family, friends and associates) since infancy. This, too, makes the path a costly one and explains why it is so difficult to talk about. It is the mystic who chooses to "sell all and follow me," the mystic who leaves father and mother in order to have his life in God.

The mystic path involves many "mini-deaths," to borrow a phrase from one of this study's participants. Gerald Heard, mystic and author, positioned those mini-deaths in language familiar to all mystics but perhaps foreign to others: "Can we ourselves hope to climb this tremendous way to the Kingdom? Certainly: there will be no Kingdom unless and until we do so climb to that station. . . . The very first step is to know that I, as I am, am an obstacle to the Kingdom. I must start, before anything else, by cleansing myself out of the way. I must learn, right down to my reflexes, to say and mean and know 'Let my name perish, so Thy Kingdom come.' "[4]

This purifying process, in which the small self is transcended, is often analogized in mystics' writings to the moth drawn to the flame which will ultimately kill it. "The lovers who dwell within the sanctuary are moths burnt with the torch of the Beloved's face,"[5] wrote a Persian mystic aglow with the impassioned love of God, attempting to describe what it is like to draw near to him. The analogy of being burned by the object of fixation is an apt one: the individual, while he is drawn toward that which is highest and best in himself, knows intuitively that he has to "die" to approach his goal.

The way involves a real and difficult crossing—not an imaginary one. The mystic wants an altered way of seeing and hearing. This necessitates, as Heard described, an obliteration of ego interests, bodily concerns, self-serving behaviors and irresponsible narcissism. Study participants who identified with the ideas of mysticism expressed their own dying-to-self in many different ways. One woman said that when she was in church, "many things I heard there lifted me out of myself," and brought out a new sense of humility.

Another vivid statement of self-transcendence came from a conversation with, and later a letter from, one of the mystics in the study: "I believe that life is reached through death. I have experienced mini-deaths before I could have room for growth. Dying to self and becoming detached from ownership, for example, helped me get close to others. In general, I saw myself wanting to detach from possessions—this might even have led me to an abandonment of ties. I've also experienced the loss of people close to me—my wife, for instance, who died two years ago—as another death for me. Through her death I was reminded of my own, not to mention the loss itself. Yet, on the other side of these experiences, I feel strongly affirmed."

In his letter following our conversation, he expanded his commentary about mini-deaths at my request: "At a recent social outing I'd dropped my cool, fallen back to stuttering and even yelled at another person in the heat of an argument. . . . [After it was over and I was apologizing] I resolved to keep myself on a higher plane and not get trapped again. But how could I tell my fiancée that the bad scene made by my 'old' self was the ground of birth for a new consciousness? I didn't even try. This was a mini-death, an inversion, a transformation."

His subsequent decision not to explain himself to his fiancée represents his dying to the ego's impulse to put itself into good standing with others, save face, protect pride. A new consciousness emerges out of that self-denying, a consciousness which—through its humility—comes closer to expressing the standards and power of the higher Self.

This transition from eccentric, self-involvement to a life lived ever more consciously through the higher aspects of personality causes the mystic—more than any other personality type—to feel as if his entire character structure is becoming undone. It is during this "undoing period" that the person often enters a "dark night of the soul," to use the familiar phrase of Saint John of the Cross. What another might interpret as alienation (from social or family support) or as not fitting in, the mystic, in his period of purgation, feels cut off from God; furthermore he cannot get solace from others because they no longer speak in language which has any meaning for him.

Saint John of the Cross wrote that there are benefits to be gained from this arid, separative period, namely that because the soul continually remembers God in its yearning for him, it is thus further purified during this lonely phase of life, becoming more capable of being one with him. His writings offer consolation to mystics who inwardly sense that no therapy, circle of helpful friends, or trusted counselor can bring relief.

> . . . from the aridities and voids of this night . . . the soul draws spiritual humility, which is the contrary virtue to the first capital sin [of] spiritual pride. . . . For it sees itself so dry and miserable that the idea never occurs to it that it is making better progress than others. . . . In this condition, souls become submissive and obedient upon the spiritual road.[6]

This passage, and its language, illustrate both the mystic's temperament and his way, and further demonstrate the concrete, transmutative nature of this life movement. The typical imagery of a mystic's vocabulary involves the words of progress, action, of movement toward or away from God: finding; searching; keeping on the way; being "stuck," lost, separated; illumination; union; arrival; completion. These kinds of words tell how mystics through the ages have experienced and verbalized their subjective sense of their own positions along their self-chosen paths.

"I'm not there yet," was a phrase I heard repeatedly from the mystics in this study. Their statement acknowledges a "location," some higher level of consciousness, to which they aspire, as well as their appraisal of their current place along the path.

A study participant had second thoughts as to whether or not she "belonged" in the study, feeling that she was so far away from the level of consciousness my questions were examining. Many weeks after our conversation she wrote this to me: ". . . maybe I do not belong in that group of persons your interesting study is about. I cannot tell myself. But since talking with you, I've thought of one theological certainty I feel I can count on. That is Albert Schweitzer's principle, presented [to me] as this: 'I am life that wills to live in the midst of other life that wills to live.' "

In a note back to her I assured her that only one who had given such reflection and time to the purpose of the study as well as to the "theological certainties" of her life would belong in our study.

Another participant, describing his own "dark night of the soul," said this: "I feel at odds with myself, cut off from conventional life yet not really connected to the Absolute. The thing that keeps me going is the memory of my previous experiences and a desire to become one with that Transcendent realm I know is real. I get glimpses of this from time to time, as if I'm seeing a friend in an alien world; these experiences give me a sense of stability, self-worth and connectedness. But there are times when I have none of that, and I just hang on in trust. . . ."

The second aspect of the mystic profile—his intense spiritual activity—is also highlighted by special language. The words the mystic uses contain a unique "invitation," a way of utilizing words to point to the awe, thanksgiving, and worshipful awareness of his highest consciousness.

Buddhists, for instance, talk of Nirvana—their "highest happiness," their union with God. The Hindus, perhaps the most lyrical mystic poets the world has produced, describe God in whispered, reverential and often boldly supernatural terms. Maher Baba, the Hindu Sadguru, described the Absolute as "the perennial spring of imperishable sweetness."[7] The Bhagavad-Gita's principal hero, Arjuna, is quoted as saying, "O boundless Form, Thou art the Primeval Diety, the Ancient Being, Thou art the Supreme Refuge of this universe; Thou art the Knower, the one to be known and the Supreme Abode. By Thee alone is this universe pervaded."[8]

Sounding much like these enraptured Orientals, yet coming from a completely different cultural tradition, Saint Thérèse of Lisieux described the mere fleeting *thought* of God in similarly ecstatic language when she said that her "heart was overflowing with love and gratitude."[9]

Jacob Boehme, an uneducated shoemaker who later was called Teutonic Theosopher, wrote, "No words can express the great joy and triumph which I experienced [i.e., while illumined with the awareness of God]. . . . While in that state, my spirit immediately saw through everything and recognized God in all things, even in herbs and grasses, and it knew what is God and what is His will. Then very soon my will grew in this light, and received a strong impulse to describe the divine state."[10]

These few examples from Eastern and Western mystical writings only skim the surface of the subjective opulence and gladness which are the mystic's as his consciousness grows saturated with the Transcendent. So closely knit are his thought and bodily responses that his God-consciousness (called, by Christians, Christ-Consciousness, and Cosmic-Consciousness by others) produces an organic, physical response in the mystic's physical body.

This is a difficult concept to convey, and our next chapter will more specifically examine the link between the mystic sense and his physical experiences or alterations to his physical state. I interviewed one physician, Dr. Lee Sannella—who has researched the physical manifestations of persons undergoing the kundalini awakening, related to Hindu meditation practices. Sannella has traced several *patterns* of bodily response to the movement of kundalini energy (psychic energy) and these are, in Sannella's research, related to intense spiritual transformation, or rebirth:

> Spiritual rebirth has become . . . a well-defined entity. . . . It is not simply an altered state of consciousness,

but an ongoing process lasting from several months to many years, during which the person passes in and out of different states of consciousness. . . . [This] can be described as an evolutionary process taking place in the human nervous system.[11]

I feel it is essential to say at this point that the mystic's passionate communication with God—his ability to transcend ordinary reality—results in experiential activity, not just in an intellectual idea of the Transcendent. He *feels* differently, sees and hears what others do not, "knows" God in a more intimate, personal way than he did before embarking upon his journey. The mystic's whole being becomes permeated with the sense and spirit of God, a phenomenon unique to those possessing the mystic sense, regardless of their cultural background. To many, the mystic borders on psychotic. Were it not for the fact that the great heroes and spiritual leaders of mankind have spoken in mystic terms it would be easy to discount their experience as insane, for their perceptions cancel out the world of the senses, the world of logic.

If we move a step further to examine the writings of those who try to describe their actual union with God, their moments of illumination, then it becomes quickly obvious they are not *able* to recount their experience coherently, so great is their joy, so disorienting their perception.

Many of the mystics in this study said, when asked about their transcendent experience, that they'd have several; few could describe them to me.

One woman did try to find the words and said this: "This is most difficult to explain because I'm not expressing myself in earth terms. At times I feel ecstatic—just imagine, if you can, the first time you fell in love. You know something wonderful is happening, something more than usual. You can *feel* it—that love emotion—welling up inside, or radiating in and out of you. At other times, it's just a great happiness that pervades my entire being. This is so hard to explain to others. And, when I'm around others who are in their normal, rather negative state, I'd rather not try—I just want to get off by myself and enjoy the exquisite, subtle state I'm in."

Another repeated the sentiment: "When I'm in that most coherent, loving state, I find it difficult to be with others—in a way it's as if I'm completely one with them; in another, it's as if what they're talking about and involved with is a pseudoreality, not real at all."

Brother Lawrence, the French lay brother of the Carmelites who lived in the 1600's, spoke of the "inexpressible sweetness," which he tasted when he communed with God.[12]

Walt Whitman, in what is perhaps the most articulate passage about the ordeal of communicating the ecstatic moment, wrote:

> When I undertake to tell the best, I find I cannot.
> My tongue is ineffectual on its pivots,
> My breath will not be obedient to its organs,
> I become a dumb man.[13]

His words reveal the mystic's intense emotional tone as well as his frustration in not being able to communicate to others what is to him highest, best, most sacred and real. This frustration itself heightens the value of self-transcendence, since the personality becomes less and less able to relate itself to others in terms of what is most meaningful. Eventually, there seems to develop a "giving up" or a greater turning in. At any rate, as others lose their position as the object of the mystic's time, attention and interest, the mystic's focus is turned progressively on a new Object on which to dwell and he experiences himself as having his whole life in Being. My sense is that there is a double-edged factor at work here: the emotion of love, as we will describe shortly, takes hold of the mystic's personality and inner being. But all is not feelings; the mystic makes a *conscious choice* to love, to have faith, to live "as if" he were in the Absolute—a choice which colors his actions and his relations with others.

Such emotions and choices further erase the old personality—a sweetly painful process which, as our study participant tried to explain, can be like falling in love. This brings us to the third element of the mystic profile: the dominance of love in his thoughts, emotions and choices.

The emotion of love, described in mystic literature of all the world, is at once painful and joyful. It has been written of as a "destructive torch . . . which opens your heart's book,"[14] or as a "burning affection of the soul which is [its] loud cry in the ears of God," or as that Love which "makes all that is heavy light and bears evenly all that is uneven."[15]

The mystic's yearning for union with God is experienced as a purifying, heated emotion which eradicates the things of old, "making all things new again." Mystic writings again and again glow with this intense, transformative ardor for the Absolute. The psalmists, prophets and poets of scriptural and mystical literature spoke of their longing for and love of God, in much the same way as did the small handful of study participants who could rightly be called mystics:

"To me," wrote the youngest study participant, age twenty-seven, "everything has meaning [because] life is a spiritual journey. My task or purpose here is to rediscover my spirituality, my relationship to God, to Truth, to the Life force in all. I want to find my way back to my own connectedness and to grow in this Truth."

Another said, "I'd have to say my 'inner program' is to realize more of the unity of life and to share that with others. This drives me totally."

Much like the good mother who wants only to give her

child the best she has even when that means self-denial and getting nothing in return, the true mystic asks for nothing from God. The mystic wishes only to give. This pure desire is in sharp contrast with the goal of lesser religions, cults and persons—referred to by Underhill as "magicians"—who wish to use their knowledge of supernatural powers to gain material possessions or personal status.

Mysticism is not an acquisitive process; it is a giving up of self. Its object is always the same: the conscious giving up of everything in order to transcend the usual physical/mental limits or excesses and have one's life in the Absolute. It is, in other words, the mystic's goal to *be* in God—not to have intellectual knowledge or special advantage over others.

This utter sincerity and "purity of heart" (to use Kierkegaard's phrase) and the willingness to abolish and annihilate the personality mark the deeply instinctive and generous quality of the mystic temperament. The Christian mystic, Meister Eckhart exemplified this posture in all his writings. He encourages those who would know God to want nothing from him:

> First let us discuss a poor man as one who wants nothing. There are some . . . who do not understand this well. They are those who are attached to their own penances and external exercises. . . . God help those who hold divine truth in such low esteem! Such people present an outward picture that gives them the name of saints; but inside they are donkeys, for they cannot distinguish divine truth. . . . So I say that a man ought to be established, free and empty, not knowing or perceiving that God is acting in him; and so a man may possess poverty.[16]

This inner emptiness is another mark of the true mystic and also corresponds to the emotion of love in its most humble, non-striving form. This emptiness is a goal of each deeply spiritual person, regardless of his cultural heritage. The Zen ideal, for instance, of emptying the mind in order to reach enlightenment is in the same spirit as Eckhart's teachings. At the moment of enlightenment Dogen-zenji, a Buddhist master, exclaimed, "There is no body and no mind!"[17] He realized in a flash that his whole being included everything in the universe, was one with All. Again echoing Eckhart's sentiments, the Zen Master Shrunryu Suzuki wrote:

> Because people have no . . . understanding of Buddha, they think what they do is the most important thing, without knowing who it is that is actually doing it . . . . Without knowing this, people put emphasis on some activity. When they put emphasis on zazen [meditation], it is not true zazen. It looks as if they were sitting in the same way as Buddha, but there is a big difference in their understanding.[18]

For the mystic, purity of intent stems from love. Indeed, it is only through love in each aspect of his life that the mystic reaches his goal. He completes his personality by giving it up. Such giving up or emptying can only be accomplished by an individual who acts out of love, who—above all else—transcends himself so as to know the One Reality.

7

Illumination and Darkness
Along the Mystic's Way

The person in the peak experience usually feels himself to be at the peak of his powers. . . . He feels more intelligent, more perceptive, wittier, stronger, or more graceful than at other times. He is at concert pitch, at the top of his form. This is not only felt subjectively but can be seen by the observer.[1] [Abraham Maslow]

The peak experience is critical to any discussion of the mystic's journey, since through it and because of it the individual gains an overarching and penetrating view into what he is at his best, into what he is when he simply *is*. The peak experience means that the person experiences himself *being* rather than becoming. He also experiences directly—and this is such a difficult point to convey to non-peakers—the Transcendent nature of reality. He enters into the Absolute, becoming one with It, if only for an instant. It is a life-altering instant which many have described as one in which the mind "stops," as a time in which the paradoxical change/changeless nature of the universe opens up to a person.

Because the insights and experiences of the peak or illuminative moment are integrative to the mind/body, we will temporarily leave our study participants and attempt to make sense out of the peak experience. This chapter is divided into three parts for the purpose of clarifying the several dimensions of the peak experience; each part deals with a specific aspect of the core-religious moment (as the illuminative moment has also been called since it is *exactly* like those private conversion experiences which serve as the foundation stones, or entry point, to all major religious traditions). The three parts of this chapter are: a general overview of the healing aspects of the peak experience, a brief comment about the reception to the mystic experience—or resistance to it—in Western culture, and finally some words about the dark side of the mystic's growth pattern.

Through the peak experience the individual gains an expanded view of himself and the world, is lifted "above" the world and his own limitations (for want of a more precise word) in a way that resolves personality splits, contradictions and blocks to full functioning. This "lifting up" of the self, this resolution of conflicts within the self, gives rise to the term *transcendence,* which, according to New Webster's Dictionary, means going beyond ordinary limits, or surpassing normal human experience. This paradox can be grasped only through the actual experience of self-transcendence, but as the words of one study participant indicate, it cultures the personality—brings out its best qualities—and heals it as well:

> [This experience] allows me to trust, to let myself accept guidance, spiritual gifts and counsel. It has let me reduce my own feelings of possessiveness and attachment. I am more relaxed, really unfidgety . . . to a degree very unusual for me. I'll go with this, in trust, and find out where this leads me.

The moment is one in which we literally "take leave of our senses," entering into a larger dimension of life—like a moment when we are completely absorbed in watching a brilliant sunset, or a time when we respond to a crisis exactly as we must in order to protect ourselves and our loved ones, perhaps watching ourselves as the actor while we do superhuman, inordinately competent things to make things right. The peak moment is a time when we come "out" of ourselves and connect with something infinite.

This *is* the moment of full, pure awareness, when the individual feels himself to be the cause of his creations *and* at the same time a part of some expansive, sacred All. This is the time of no-duality. During this moment, the person is most innocent, childlike, spontaneous, vulnerable, unguarded, defenseless and open. He is all these things because his separateness (that which, in a previous chapter, one of the study participants linked to "insanity") has ended; he is bonded to a unitive force. This bonding creates—in consciousness and in the physical body as well—feelings of worthiness, compassion, love, of being responsible, capable, fully able to do. And, as this chapter's opening quote and the one that follows suggest, he also appears that way to others:

> [In the peak-experience, the person is] more apt to give the impression that it would be useless to try to stop him. It is as if now he had no doubts about his worth, or about his ability to do whatever he decided to do. To the observer he looks more trustworthy, more reliable, more dependable, a better bet. It is often possible to spot this great moment of becoming responsible—in therapy, in growing up, in education, in marriage.[2]

The instance bestows on an individual the sense that all of creation is wonderful, God-filled, orderly and safe. Fears dissolve into nothing, as if they had never existed, as if they were a lie, a delusion. This sense of safety (which also includes the individual being ridden of the fear of death) provides yet another key to why the peak experience heals so profoundly, since much neuroticism thrives on nameless fears and vague, free-floating anxieties.

During, and usually after, the illuminative moment, the individual perceives everything as brighter, clearer, richer, more lustrous. This lustrous and expanded perceptual field is etched ever after in the individual's mind, and this further fuels the mystic's path, even enhances the individual's ability to recall and *use* the experience for his personal growth.

In fact, my rather radical suggestion is that an individual can't reach full personality health until, and unless, he has had a peak-experience, until he has transcended his own limited self, and met himself in and as *being*. It is very likely that those who have the "cosmic sense" (either through a sudden, intense conversion experience or through an almost constant, gradual and lesser dose of peak experiences) are healthier people than the norm.

Whatever their faults may be, these persons are likely to be more autonomous, integrated, open and fully developed than people who haven't transcended, who cannot recall such moments or who actively resist the idea. The phenomenon is so closely joined to creativity and what is currently called "right brain thinking" that it would be hard to discuss either of these attributes without also presenting information on the peak experience.

Richard Bucke, a physician who extensively studied and catalogued the personality traits of those he felt had "cosmic consciousness," found that his subjects shared several exemplary traits: they were morally elevated, were intellectually illumined, had a sense of their own immortality, and had lost their fear of death as well as their sense of sin. Each had had one or more sudden "awakening" experiences, and their personality had that added charm which made them so attractive to others. His description of their appeal to others sounds remarkably like Maslow's observation of the personality of the peaker.

Of Walt Whitman, someone with a supremely well developed mystic sense, Bucke wrote:

> When I first knew Walt Whitman I used to think that he watched himself, and did not allow his tongue to give expression to feelings of fretfulness, antipathy, complaint and remonstrance. . . . After long observation . . . I satisfied myself that such absence or unconsciousness was entirely real. His deep, clear and earnest voice [contributed to] the charm of the simplest things he said. . . . He never spoke deprecatingly of any nationality or class of men, or time in the world's history . . . or against any trades or occupations—not even against any animals, insects, plants or inanimate things, nor any of the laws of nature, nor any of the results of the laws, such as illness, deformity or death. He never complained or grumbled either at the weather, pain, illness or anything else. He never in conversation . . . used language that could be considered indelicate. . . . He never spoke in anger . . . never exhibited fear, and I do not believe he ever felt it.[3]

Some of the people in this study fit (although perhaps in lesser degrees) Bucke's catalogue of traits of the cosmically conscious. They have had, and frequently "enter," the peak experience—as we shall see in the chapter with case study interviews. Their primary interest is the Absolute, the values of Being-cognition, and—like Whitman and others in Bucke's research—they never complained, grumbled, or spoke of needing any "thing" to round out their happiness and make it full.

Subjects like truth, justice, beauty, the Absolute or Transcendent state are of high interest to them, and they express a desire to live life in a way that exemplifies the qualities of that

which is highest and best in them. It is as if their lives have
become imprinted with the qualities experienced during, and
gained through, self-transcendence. In varying degrees, they
express a loss of fear (e.g., fear of death, of scarcity, of what-
will-others-say, or of defying convention). Of this, one study
participant wrote me a letter in which he states: "How can we
experience the scriptural teaching, 'Perfect love casts out fear'?
The full range of human fears has at its center the fear of death.
Each time we succumb to a fear we experience a little death,
and through each overcoming of a fear we are reborn. More
fully, the conquest of fear is analogous to dying in that we risk
losing in the process and gain a new life as the result."

The peak experience conditions the personality to death
because during it, the individual "ego" (i.e., separate sense,
the "I") vanishes. With this vanishing goes the fear of death,
since the ego, the I, is what keeps those fears in place, believing
as it does that there is a death—that is to say, a no-life condition—to fear. When the personality joins something so much
larger, eternal, infinite—even with the disappearance of the
separate sense of self—the fear of death goes.

Some of the study participants remarked that their peak
experiences had awakened them to something which was so
much more than they had ever known previously.

One woman wrote, "I have had many awareness experiences of transcendence. These have changed my life in that I
felt I touched the depth of existence, the incredible. I've retained a sense of awe, as well as the knowledge that 'It' is there
if I can learn to be open enough, trusting enough."

Another woman, in her seventies, said, "At the age of
eighteen I had several peak spiritual experiences which transformed my life. These have caused me to take positive action
toward a definite life's direction—[as a result] my life's philosophy is tied to a real sense of God. Since college my life's verse

has been summed up by Deuteronomy 33:27, 'The eternal God is my dwelling place, and underneath are the everlasting arms.' "

Another said, "An out-of-body experience which I had in 1976 changed my life. It made me more aware of inner images, urgings and intuitions. Since then I have leaned on these aspects of myself when making decisions and life-choices." His comments remind us of the opening remarks about wholeness: that wholeness comes to whoever finds out what is, for him, good and holds fast to that. The peak-experience, according to study participants, opens the way to their discovery of inner truths and "the good."

The study participants' perceptual sense of abundance increased. They speak about experiencing the world around them as luscious and full. They commented how odd it was, given their materially sparse life situations (sparse by their own standards as well as society's), to feel so rich.

This isn't puzzling once we grasp that the peak experience expands the individual's field of consciousness to include everything in the universe: he feels he *has* everything because he experiences everything within. Maharishi Mahesh Yogi has repeatedly taught that this experience opens the individual up to the "field of all possibilities." This field is what author Joseph Chilton Pearce calls the "crack in the cosmic egg." Although Pearce is also talking about the *metanoia*—the transformation of an individual's entire belief system which accompanies the peak experience or moment of illumination—he writes of the exquisite insight which makes "all things new again," the unifying, integrative moment which provides the individual with a glimpse of the connectiveness of all things—the micro/macro web of the universe, interrelationships of all people and things. This is a way of "seeing" which has no dualities, a way of perceiving that shows us we are born, have our lives and "die" within the context of a comprehensible, coherent, intelligent whole—a whole which loses nothing even though everything is always changing.

In this moment, the individual is taken out of himself and becomes disconnected from rigid, scientific or culturally-created laws. He becomes one with everything, loses his feelings of desperation and feels a deep, healing inner peace and harmony.

A study participant commented about his own healing: "My transcendent experiences continue to transform my life over and over again, like reverberations that don't end. I've come to accept the fluidity of my life. I'm learning to live a life of faith, trusting I'll be provided for—not in a passive way, of course, but in a way that fears less and less. My work [i.e., as a result of these experiences] becomes 'proving' God in every action, every event, even in the difficulties of life. Not I but Thou, because ultimately, there's nowhere else to turn. The union of this sort, [which I've carried with me since self-transcendence] is healing. What creates insanity is separation."

The individual who has [or in rarer cases, as our case studies in Chapter 8 describe, who lives in] this moment is liberated from the narrow confines of ordinary waking consciousness. As a result, his energy, intensity, focus and elation are greatly enhanced. For some, this is a once-in-a-lifetime glimpse of what they are at their deepest level of being, a glimpse which changes them forevermore. For others, these times come repeatedly. For those with a natural propensity toward mysticism (and not all those who have the peak-experience have this propensity or leaning) this instant is their introduction to infinity, their life-altering initiation into the cosmic sense.

The poet, artist and mystic William Blake likened this condition of mind, heart and perception to the cleaning of our perceptual field. In his now classic verse from *The Marriage of Heaven* (classic no doubt because his words in articulate language helped frame that ineffable moment which scores of others experience but cannot explain clearly) he writes:

> If the doors of perception were cleansed, everything would appear to man as it is, infinite. For man has closed himself up, till he sees all thro' the narrow chinks of his cavern.[4]

At the very least, the peak experience widens the individual's perception so that he "sees" something larger, so that his own little personality fuses itself to an eternal, infinite state of consciousness.

Maslow called the peak experience an "acute identity experience." By this he meant that the individual becomes himself in a pure and uncontaminated way, that he feels himself to be boundless, at one with the world, at peace with himself, simultaneously powerful and vulnerable. For the moment his logical, culturally-conditioned mind and personality, his time/space orientation become suspended, and self-consciousness dissolves to a new paradigm of Self-awareness. The individual in the peak-experience is always liberated, "free," or—some would say—enlightened, illumined, full of light. He is unconstricted and spontaneous, yet completely focused and totally present in the moment.

Maslow believed that the world could be divided into two "religions": peakers and non-peakers. Of this division he said that some people can't admit to having had a core or peak experience and subsequently can't use such experiences to further their own development. He believed that these people were constitutionally different, "with a profound characterological makeup" which was completely at odds with the character structure of peakers. His writings suggest that non-peakers either deny, repress or perhaps never have had peak experiences. He proposed that LSD or other similar drugs might stimulate such experiences in non-peakers, thus closing the gap between these two dissimilar types of human beings:

> In the last few years it has become quite clear that certain drugs called "psychedelic," especially LSD and psilocybin, give us some possibility of control in this realm of peak experiences. . . . Perhaps we can actually produce a private personal peak experience under observation and whenever we wish under religious or non-religious circumstances . . . [thus bridging the gap] between these two separated halves of mankind.[5]

My own observations, which I'll expand upon shortly, indicate two primary dangers in using such drugs. First, the long-term effects of psychedelic drugs may actually deprive people of the motivation to grow and to function in a way that is best for their highest happiness. The effects of such drugs may render a person ultimately so lethargic, perhaps for just a time, that he will not seek out the very experiences—rigorous as these might be—he needs in order to confront his self-imposed limits in the proper way and thus grow. Second, in my opinion, there is still an unexplained connection between the human nervous system, the individual's ability to experience transcendence, and his world-view as a whole. I'm not yet convinced that the long-range effects of any drugs on the human nervous system can produce the effects Maslow hoped for.

Also, as an educator who has seen countless people—children, young adults and adults—at different levels of learning and experience, I find it somewhat intolerant, perhaps even insulting, to another to require that he take a drug to experience what I do.

Moreover, at its core, my professional view about peakers vs. non-peakers is different than Maslow's. While I also meet many men and women who do not recall having had a peak experience (denying, repressing, or simply not having had them), my sense is that this lack is itself symptomatic of a *stage* of personal development, not a division of *types* of humans, not evidence that the person is characterologically or constitutionally different.

This view is in keeping with the Eastern (in this case, Hindu) idea of levels of consciousness. The conceptual framework I have in mind and which is helpful to this issue goes this way: all humans experience three basic levels of consciousness: waking, dreaming and dreamless sleep. The fourth level, pure awareness—what I have been calling transcendence or the peak experience, and some might say these are different—is gained suddenly during prayer, meditation or some unexpected, creative or leisurely moment. The fifth stage, what Bucke called "cosmic consciousness," is reached when the fourth state of transcendent awareness is *retained* along with the three other relative states. In Chapter 8, one of the case study interviewees describes this fourth state quite nicely for us. The two highest states of consciousness are God-consciousness, wherein the individual experiences ever-subtler grades of transcendent thought during his ordinary daily and dream consciousness, and finally Unity-consciousness, in which the individual's nervous system *and* regular consciousness are so highly developed that the person lives *in* total unity with the Absolute.

Each of these states is a logical consequence of the one that precedes it. For instance, the mystic state would flow naturally out of the fourth stage—the transcendent level of consciousness. This framework, which until recently has been lacking in the Western tradition, is to me elegant and orderly in several ways, especially in terms of understanding peak-experiencers and mystics.

First, under this system of thinking, a peak-experiencer is not necessarily a mystic. The person who has had one, or several, peak experiences may not be moved to search for a repeat of this experience or to spend his entire life searching for God. Many great artists, athletes, mothers, executives and scientists show the *effects* of self-transcendence (and even in their comments acknowledge having had such moments) but may not be moved to do anything more but use the insights gained to become the best person they can be within the context of their own professions and their own lives. I'm not sure that the mystic desire for oneness with God gives him a corner on being a "better" person, or a higher species, and suppose the key would be in the "fruits" of his desires, the outcomes of his life. Mystics, by definition, dedicate their lives to striving for union with the Transcendent; the peak experience fuels and energizes their desires, while in most it just enriches, heals and makes more whole their life.

Second, a mystic can attain a highly developed cosmic sense and still have a way to go in his development. Returning to peakers and non-peakers, my feeling (at this stage in my research and understanding) is that the more highly developed the personality the more likely it is that the individual will be able to have and remember a peak experience. The more open he will be to ideas—including the idea of an orderly, abundant universe, the interrelationship of all life, and the acceptance of the concept of infinity.

In my professional practice where I deal primarily with well-educated, bright and ambitious executives (especially creative, entrepreneurial types) I find that most are reasonably open to discussing such issues once they trust the person they're speaking to. Even the most rational, linear thinkers can be gently encouraged to recall such experiences, since there are many common life instances that provide access to the peak moment—such as in sports, when concentrating on a complex, fascinating problem and then totally relaxing (the subsequent leisure time often giving rise to the peak moment, the "aha" experience in which insights and an answer sought after naturally comes into the mind), or even during a sexual experience, where the moment of orgasm is often likened to a peak-experience in that the individual ego is momentarily dissolved.

A client of mine, a lawyer with whom I regularly visit (and as bright, ethical and sensitive a man as one could hope to meet), reacted skeptically when I first mentioned my interest in mysticism and peak experiences. He said that he had never had a peak experience, and that he felt that only "emotional types" cared about such matters. Knowing he was an avid skier, I asked him if—while skiing—he'd ever had a time when he'd been so totally absorbed in the activity that he'd forgotten all work, cares and fears and had joined into the skiing in so highly an involved way that he actually *became* the skiing. He remembered having many such experiences, and broke out in a big smile, saying that he hadn't realized that that was what it had been. He added that these moments were, for him, the best moments of his life, times of incredible happiness, balance and focus. He commented that during those times, he was so fully absorbed in the activity that he—his personality, his cares, his goals and so on—seemed to vanish, bringing him into a sense of tremendous power and freedom.

Whatever the person's life-interests, this is exactly the outcome of the peak experience: the individual becomes egoless, perceives a kind of perfection in and around him, and self-transcends in a way that clarifies and makes all things whole. These moments bring people true happiness. They feel justified in some way, as if life has expanded meaning and elegance. Of his skiing episodes, my client said that he had felt renewed afterward, and wondered if that was why, when he had had too much work and worldly pressures, he headed for the ski slopes. If he was too busy to ski, just remembering his experiences on the slopes refreshed him.

In fact, the feeling of renewal often continues long after the peak experience. Transcenders can, and regularly do, enter into the memory of their egoless times whenever they feel the need to be refreshed. Something cleansing, organizing and stress-releasing happens to the entire mind/body through these experiences. It is this cleansing—coupled with a cluster of perceptual changes (such as *being* more responsive, holistic and synergistic rather than just *thinking* about these values)—which contributes greatly to personality health.

In spite of all the benefits of the illuminative moment described above, the Western world has long been closed to this type of experience. The great prophets and seers in every major religion have probably all had a core-religious experience. Yet little is said about such matters in the traditional church environment. Almost every Judeo-Christian element has its highly organized, legalistic and dogmatic aspect, within which a smaller, essentially spiritual element exists. Usually this spiritual core is just a handful of unorganized, unconnected individuals, whose prayer life so richly contributes to their ability to have an intimate personal relationship with God that they could be called mystics. These private persons—whose spiritual experiences are likely to be revelatory, transcendent, illuminative—may belong to any of the great world religions or may not be part of any religious structure.

But overall, our Western culture—with some exceptions, primarily stemming from the Catholic monastic traditions, the more liberal elements within the Episcopal Church, some evangelical movements which stress the healing, transformative power of the Holy Spirit, and a few psychoanalytic schools (e.g., Jungian, Assagioli and the Transpersonal Schools, etc.)—remains uniquely closed to the subject of mysticism and the higher reaches of human, transpersonal consciousness.

On the macro level of the larger society, our relatively young culture has only recently become sufficiently developed to entertain such ideas. Also, the teaching of the Church after the Middle Ages contributed to a long-lasting negative attitude about mysticism.

During the early period of the Church, through at least the first decade after Christ, the religious traditions encouraged contemplative, personal religious experiences. An intimate, direct relationship with God—an experiential relationship, which I'll assume would have been a level of consciousness open to transcending—was what Saint Paul must have been referring to when he talked about *knowing* God. His own conversion experience was sudden, and transformed his entire life's course. After it, Paul frequently urged his disciples to grow in their own intimate knowledge of God.[6]

This positive tradition of the contemplative knowledge of the Absolute continued through the Middle Ages, when medieval monks practiced a somewhat "methodless" prayer in which they repeated scriptural passages, listening to their words as they said them, and entering into these sacred phrases with their entire bodies as well as with their minds. Monks memorized many passages of Scripture since there was no printing, therefore no books. This vocal or sub-vocal prayer was their life-changing response to God and represented their direct, meditative discourse with him, as do chanting and other liturgical prayers today.

In this way, they were transported physically and mentally—i.e., experientially, rather than just intellectually—into close, personal communion with God.

During these decades prayer, contemplation and meditation were woven together into one undivided way of communing with God. These three acts could be engaged in during the same prayer session, and frequently resulted in a kind of resting *in* God—much as in Eastern meditation in which the individual transcends his personal boundaries to join the Absolute.

Around the twelfth century, however, things began to change. With the birth of many new schools of theology and a more precise, analytical approach to prayer and religious practices came an increase in the tendency to classify, analyze and compartmentalize prayer life, and a decline in contemplative prayer. As the centuries rolled on, mental prayer was further classified and divided into discursive, affective or mystical depending on whether the individual's prayer time was dominated by his thoughts, acts of will or the graces of God respectively. Now three separate acts were no longer combined into a single prayer session. Rather, contemplation during prayer time seemed unlikely (no wonder, given all the attention to thinking about what type of prayer one was doing) and was even presented as something "dangerous."

The compartmentalization of prayer into different types, the idea that contemplation was reserved for a very few, that it might even be full of danger and not something to which the ordinary Christian should aspire, were all factors which eroded mystical theology during the sixteenth and seventeenth centuries.

> The final nail that was hammered into the coffin of the traditional teaching of the Church was the obvious corollary that it was against humility to aspire to contemplation. . . . As devout people moved spontaneously into [the normal contemplative view of truth during prayer] they were up against this very negative attitude. They hesitated to go beyond discursive meditation because of instructions or warnings they were given about the dangers of mysticism. They either gave up mental prayer altogether, or, through the mercy of God, found some way of persevering in spite of the obstacles.[7]

This brief overview may help explain why there's been a general inattention, if not outright skepticism, to the potentials inherent in the mystic state of consciousness. Not until Maslow codified the benefits of the peak experience, as well as what he called the Being-values (i.e., values which correspond to the awareness of the transcendent realm), did researchers, educators and the various helping professions begin paying closer attention to the attitudes, behaviors and values of human health. As I've mentioned periodically in this book, the helping professions are—in my observation and experience—still tied much too closely, in their own awareness and expectation, to lesser values: to fear, phobias, limitations, the "coping" needs of human beings who manufacture, or are at the effect of their own, problems and negativity. Their modality of advice-giving, the frame of reference of their own professional biases, are those of "adjusting" to a culturally-defined set of problems, and not geared to introducing people to their transpersonal, higher selves. Of course, this is a generality, and there is a new-wave of psychologists, physicians and other health-care professionals who concern themselves with health, personal choice, responsible action. They are still in the minority, surrounded by others who—by their own perceptions—present a limited set of options to their clients and patients.

As we have seen, some authors (such as Underhill and Bucke) have suggested that only the mystic can be called whole—awakened to the hidden powers of an otherwise sleeping portion of the self. That may be true, largely because as described the experience of awakening so profoundly impacts a person's well-being and self-view, the expression of his best self.

But awakening the "sleeping portions of the self" has a dark side. People who stretch the limits of their consciousness and nervous systems may experience many psychological and even physical discomforts.

During much of the early stages of the mystic path, the personality moves sporadically toward a higher, more expanded limit of its own consciousness. This invariably involves the individual's nervous systems, since images, ideas and altered—even if pleasurable—states of consciousness affect the mind/body—the whole physiological biosphere.

The individual is pushing into a newly developed, unexplored and highly private zone of experience. At the very least, the most tender emotions are tapped—as well as the most fearsome ones. The person can feel inordinately sad, vulnerable or moved. He can be touched instantly by waves of strong emotions at little or no provocation.

One person in this study told me that during a meeting, for no apparent reason, some heroic quality in a colleague so moved him that he had to fight back tears. Another said that he had had long periods of time when he couldn't participate in social situations, such was his need for solitude, privacy and quiet. Yet another reported feeling very vulnerable, much like the feelings she had had when her child was born when she didn't want other people near the baby. She said, "I feel very tender inside, as if I want to protect myself against negativity, smallness of mind, as if I'm incubating something within. . . . I intuitively know this won't last, but right now I have a lot of difficulty being with people."

The Western tradition—our schools, social institutions, helping professionals, and all their training support systems, our churches and synagogues—have very little empathy for solitude. The "togetherness" banner has been strung over every social institution: families are taught they must do everything together, marriages are built on the foundation of constant time together (with no options for either spouse to spend time alone, as if time alone was a mark of a failing marriage), children are encouraged to socialize continually, having very little encouragement or practice in spending time alone, corporations (a set of systems I'm very familiar with) often are punitive with managers or lower level employees who want to spend time by themselves (lunches, coffee breaks, dinners out are all times to socialize with others)—our whole cultural set-up is geared to interactive time. Little wonder that when an individual starts to grow within himself, starts to develop his intuitive, transpersonal self, he may find it necessary to pull back, to learn how to be alone.

Moreover, the Western tradition has few role models for those going through the turmoils of inner growth, even though common sense tells us that whenever anyone extends themselves into the farther reaches of his own awareness, awakening to what is deepest and most sacred within—with his own unique abysses, dreams and nightmarish images, memories, aspirations—he may suffer a subtle and a devastating level of unexplainable stress. I call this stress "extension stress," and define it as the wear-and-tear within the mind/body/nervous system of someone who is reaching toward a level of awareness *and* functioning to which he is not yet adapted.

Extension stress (and really this is only an adjustment of the definition of "distress" which researcher Hans Selye gave us many years ago) can be compared with the stresses suffered by those rare, unusual Olympic athletes who push their minds and bodies to the outer limits so that their physical performances can reach new heights. With such goals they must convince themselves that their body can do what they demand. The person who desires self-transcendence—who spends long hours in meditation, reflection, prayer about issues that bring psychic rebirth—faces a good deal of pain. This pain might come from any number of sources: from the opening of inner sensibilities and reflecting on an entire life (including the refinement of habits, behaviors, relationships with others) and from letting go, as we have described in previous chapters, of culturally-ingrained ideas, possessions, aspirations. Letting go is a loss, and all loss carries with it grief work, stresses which take a long time to work through, questions about our choices and actions.

The person who starts this work from the point of view of an Eastern tradition has a time-honored and more detailed road-map to follow, as well as gurus, teachers, symbolism and language that makes this type of pain more understandable. However, in the West—with our emphasis on competition, social and personal gratification, a psychoanalytic, parenting and educational tradition which encourages "adjustment" rather than actualization (actualization is often interpreted as "Me-ism" by the press who gets its language from marketing experts and book-promoting newsmakers from any number of professions)—there is a strong tendency to view any inner turmoil (especially that which comes from a self-imposed inner journey) as neurotic anxiety or selfishness or imaginary hypochondria.

Fortunately, increasing attention is being given to thinkers who acknowledge the difficulties faced by those undergoing this most sincere and radical transformation. Thomas Merton suggests that there is an existential anxiety crisis that precedes the final integration of life as a "new man."[8] He tells us that this anxiety is a necessary partner to psychic rebirth, the birth of the person into a higher level of functioning and perceiving and feeling. This final integration, because it demands a state of functioning and maturity beyond mere social adjustment, creates the cosmic or universal man:

> He has gained a deeper, fuller identity than that of his limited ego-self which is only a fragment of his being. . . . He has attained to a deep inner freedom—the Freedom of the Spirit we read about in the New Testament. . . . Now, this calls to mind the theology of St. Thomas on the Gifts of the Holy Spirit which move a man to act in a "superhuman mode."[9]

The anxieties which must be faced while en route to such a personality are painful and more dangerous than the anxieties born of ordinary life as we know it. Saint John of the Cross felt that any separation from God was like a "dark night." He passed through a period of intense inner discomfort—feeling troubled, resisting his spiritual work, feeling as if "devils" were assaulting him at every turn. Merton suggests that today anyone undergoing the final integration of actualization (although he doesn't refer to it as "actualization") would soon (if discovered) find himself getting shock treatments, which would effectively take care of any further disturbing developments.

One of the study participants described his own "dark night" this way: "I was bereft, having started on a path I knew nothing about, having left all my old friends, key members of my family, feeling totally alone. I could remember flashes of experiences where I'd felt myself to be one with the Absolute, experiences which had encouraged me in a way no social or material accomplishment ever had. Yet I was cut off from those experiences. I felt I had no options—not one way to go that could help; not even suicide was open to me, believing as I do that when you take your own life there are unresolved issues you'll have to deal with at another time, in another way. All I could do was wait. The waiting, as painful as it was and as disturbed as I was, strengthened me, deepened my faith. I found in my waiting that the demands placed upon me prompted a response from me—that my own responding to life's demands was a source of hope for me. That was really all I had, my ability to respond. But it helped me through a most difficult time. It deepened my faith."

The language of Sufism offers us a sacred term called *Fana*, meaning the annihilation of the self, a spiritual death. This death is followed by *Baga*, the reintegration of the personality. It is this period, the inner solitude, loneliness and perhaps even despair which creates the emotional, often the physical, ills I am speaking about which our society so poorly understands and cannot tolerate.

The Eastern tradition has always acknowledged that the rebirth process—including self-annihilation, the reintegration of personality—is painful. The Zen tradition, for example, in keeping with its rather intellectual, unemotional observer's stance regarding all attachment, acknowledges such pain but instructs its followers to detach from any physical or mental discomfort—as well as pleasure—as just something else to relinquish on the path to Satori.

Hindu schools talk about *kundalini*, which we have described earlier as an energy residing (or sleeping) at the base of the spine which begins its awakening when the individual starts the rebirth process through selected meditative techniques. When this energy awakens it can create havoc in the central nervous system, according to believers, until it has worked its way up the spinal column, removing all blocks and stresses as it goes. This belief may or may not be "true." Still it is a legacy, a sort of rite of passage, for growth and helps explain, deal with and conceptualize the rebirth process.

Gopi Krishna, who charted his experiences in his autobiography, *Kundalini,* describes one incident in which the *kundalini* was moving in his body, a time when he thought he was going to die:

> The heat [from the fiery currents that darted through my body] grew every moment, causing such unbearable pain that I writhed and twisted from side to side while streams of cold perspiration poured down my face and limbs. But still the heat increased. . . . Suffering the most excruciating torture . . . there were dreadful disturbances in all the organs, each so alarming and painful that I wonder how I managed to retain my self-possession. . . . The whole delicate organism was burning, withering away completely under the fiery blast racing through its interior.[10]

Western medicine is slow to realize that merely a change in thought can affect the physical body, for better or worse. It has "discovered" that the brain, as the largest gland in the body, emits specific hormones depending on the type of idea the thinker holds in his head—that ideas are *things* in the body which have the power to create life or death. It isn't surprising that people who consciously choose to disintegrate their old selves—their egocentricity, culturally/parentally-conditioned selves and who risk the challenges of solitary life during the disintegration period—might undergo emotional and even physical crisis.

I am, at this writing, unable to explain some of the phenomena I have witnessed (in the study participants and in myself) as clearly as I might wish. For example, often in those who have used psychedelic drugs to induce their peak experiences I have observed an indecisiveness or passivity. One study participant compared this to "living in glue." This observation, and I have seen it many times, gives rise to my conservative stance on the use of drugs to create peak experiences which I described at length earlier. In these persons, the nervous system seems blocked, robbed of energy, under-stimulated in a way that creates *inaction* and the inability to *decide* which way to go in a host of simple life choices. It may be that what the person describes as lethargy is simply his body's specific response to the type of transformation he desires—radical inner growth, "death" and reintegration. In this case, it is likely that energy once available for work, social relations and creative effort is now redirected toward exploring the frontiers of consciousness at heretofore unexamined levels. On the other hand, it may also be that the nervous system is exhausted, over-taxed—either because of drugs or because it hasn't yet adapted to the new faculty of consciousness being sought. I should add that I've also seen people "grow out of" their apathy, eventually returning to more self-expressive, active states—what they call "normal functioning." Still, this is an area that needs much more examination, research and clarification.

Our society now needs more physicians sympathetic to this type of issue, physicians who can help humanity understand the physiological dynamic of transcendence. We need guides—clerics, counselors, therapists—who know something about the final integration phase of self-realization, persons who know—first-hand—about the rebirth and transpersonal maturity which the self-transcendent person seeks. Too many therapists, psychoanalysts and physicians are either unfamiliar with or unfriendly toward spiritual topics, tend to see everything as pathology and treat every problem as disease. Similarly, our Judeo-Christian tradition—unlike the various Eastern schools mentioned earlier—has not been inclined to depend on spiritual masters or teachers for human development needs. Perhaps this is a blessing in disguise; certainly we do not need yet another institutionalized set of rules, certificates and courses to assist people with what is basically a highly personal, individualized matter.

It is certain, with all I have said about our culture needing to sensitize itself to the spiritual dimension of life, that many great geniuses, mystics and saints—such as Walt Whitman, William Blake, Mother Teresa, Buckminster Fuller, and countless others—have had the inner resources to foster their own growth, in spite of society's obstacles. However, many more—*ordinary* people with ordinary levels of intelligence, or unglamorous occupations, etc.—could possibly be encouraged toward healthier self-development, toward self-transcendence, if schools, churches and other social institutions were sympathetic to the values of this work. They could discover that life is much more than "making do" and adjusting to the expectations of others. For that to happen, our society must place as much emphasis on spiritual growth as it places on other aspects of individual accomplishment.

8

The Mystic's Consciousness:
Three Case Studies

> Q. If you were to describe to another the personal at-
> tributes which have helped you to be happy, pro-
> ductive and contributive, what would you say these
> were?
>
> A. Acceptance. Creativity. Perseverance. Inspiration.
> Hunger for the Divine. [Study Participant, Califor-
> nia]

The case studies which follow represent three examples of mystic consciousness. These adults meet many, if not all, of the
criteria of the mystic described in earlier chapters. Each has a
decided "hunger for the Divine," each has the ability to have,
recall and use his or her peak experiences; each continues to
grow in his or her mystic sense while at the same time expressing several of the key attributes of mysticism: sense of being
interrelated to others and to the universe, the loss of fears and
need for "things," or striving, the emotion of love.

Each person speaks of, and, to a great extent, exhibits in
daily life, the cosmic or unitive consciousness which I have spoken about in the last two chapters. Each perceives that he or
she lives in an integrated, interrelated, "friendly" world, having either totally or partially extinguished the fear of death—

117

as well as other nameless fears—which torments most people. Each is functioning effectively, self-sufficiently, in a role natural to his or her own talents, while simultaneously retaining the Transcendent realm in consciousness.

The first case study, that of a researcher and bibliographer, demonstrates the ongoing yearning, the heart hunger and absorption for the Absolute which are characteristic of the true mystic.

The second case, a housewife and mother, demonstrates the goal-less, non-striving nature of the completed personality—the personality that experiences itself as needing nothing more to be happy, as needing no "added thing" for its fulfillment. I particularly liked this interview because the study participant expresses a fully-rounded happiness which contradicts a standard expectation of many professionals in the mental-health field. (I recall one lecture I heard recently where the speaker, a psychologist and minister, told the audience that the adult personality always felt incomplete, that only persons ready to die could feel satisfied with life, could be goal-less. It is just this sort of misinformation which mental-health care professionals keep feeding the public—a type of malnourishment which then deprives them of models for happiness.)

The third case study, that of a writer and poet, illustrates the fully developed mystic type with its artistic, intense temperament, and aesthetic, passionate interest in spiritual matters, its strongly marked, intimate experience of and relationship to God. It was gratifying to me to meet this participant, particularly because most of the texts about enlightenment make it seem as though the enlightened individual is a rarity, someone who must travel to far-off lands or study for years and years with gurus in order to be self-realized. The participant's comments and—more than that—his utter simplicity of manner and life-style, the total unassuming quality of his environment, words, way of seeing things, lets each of us see that self-realization, self-transcendence, actualization can be ours; it may be a grace—but it can be ours. One of the persons is an active member of an organized religion. The other two—though highly spiritual and sensitive to godly issues—are not church-goers; if anything they are—like so many of the study participants—turned off to organized religion. As one of the study participants put it, "You can't organize the Truth."

My interpretation of their reluctance to participate in, or perhaps even relate to, organized religion is similar to Maslow's. Through the ages, the mystic's experience happens individually, not institutionally, not under the auspices of an organized, structured setting. Maslow pointed out that religious organizations often *spring up around,* and are designed to structure, communicate and legitimize, the illumination, conversion experience of an individual. It is often very difficult for the true mystic to find rapport with such institutions, his own heightened sensitivities to God made profane by the mundane perceptions of those who want to hear about—but who themselves do not *experience*—the sacred reverence and humility of the Transcendent.

At the same time, those who are religiously inclined, who do belong to and support an organized religion, who do go to church regularly, usually, as a result of their self-transcendence, become *more* devout, more strengthened in their faith. I suspect that these are highly individualized answers, that each person who is mystically inclined experiences the Absolute in his own way, much as revelation itself is highly unpredictable and individual.

Each case study is presented with a slightly different emphasis simply because my own conversations and correspondence with each person was unique, taking shape from the person's own interests and comments. In a manner typical to my professional practice, where I interview many people each week, I joined the study participants where they were—i.e., entered their world, their reality—rather than asking them to join me in mine. In one case, the first case study, I had to interview the participant over the phone; the phone conversations were followed by his several letters to me. In the case of the other two, I met them at their homes for a rather lengthy in-person talk. Fortunately, each is articulate, a patient teacher, and easy to understand.

Case Study # 1
Researcher, Bibliographer (Male)

This participant lives in the south as a "hermit in the woods." He is in his fifties, and left suburbia when his wife— now deceased—and sons began looking for a wilderness site on which to live. His small cabin has no utilities, no running water. His mail-order business is run largely by battery-operated computers. "I go 'out' three times a week, and enjoy the solitude, trying (not always efficiently) to conduct my business as a service for people looking for inaccessible books," he wrote in one letter.

Of his own growth, his solitary life and work he said:

"For years I was unconsciously seeking approval from other people, wanting them to tell me I'm all right. Now I see that this sort of assurance is irrelevant, even if it were possible: that in assuming others were 'all right' but being uncertain of myself, my misunderstanding of them was as complete as my misunderstanding of myself. In truth I wasn't all right, and no one's sanction could change this.

"So what happened? Within the bounds of respectability, I had developed some goals (which are still before me), but made a string of botched attempts at life and working.

[Note: He—the larger Self—is now able to comment with

openness on the fearfulness of his previous self, without need to defend himself, a sign that the fears and the sense of inadequacy are dissolving.]

"For living, solitude is perhaps best for me, and for work my computer is the effective solution. Regarding work, I've lived all my life with books. . . . I've realized the extensive monograph and lists which I've accumulated has potential to be of much help to others.

"It's much more difficult to write about life. Basically, we do not see the whole picture. From birth we perceive it through the gates of our physical senses and are taught to instill those responses which are culturally 'correct.' It is hard work to question those imposed interpretations and attempt to establish our own. Two key insights which I'm reaching have to do with change and death: we are temporary, in process; and we shall die. Accordingly, we can see and touch nothing that is fixed, changeless, absolute. First, one realizes that everything is relative, maybe later on that everything is related. . . . From here it is a short step to a sense of stewardship: I have the responsibility of caring for what is entrusted to me and of limiting my acquisitions of more than I need. . . .

"It is an illusion to suppose that any security can be found on earth: the only security is trust in God. . . . After half a century and much struggle to discern, I believe it to be true of the human situation. Much of the disorder that we see in other people comes from confused priorities and from attempts to be in control.

[Note: here he illustrates the growing sense of interrelationship and stewardship born of loving the other, of complete identification with the other-as-self.]

"I'm slowly learning that other people are basically like me. I can assume that the deep 'self' of another person will answer (if he or she is able to respond freely) whenever I am expecting to discover a brother or sister. These discoveries affirm this depth in me and reinforce this growing sense of who people are.

"... the only adequate answer I know is that we are all being called to become brothers and sisters in Christ."

Of his experience with self-transcendence, he said:

"My earliest experience was when I was about fifteen and saw Van Gogh's "Crows Over a Cornfield," in an exhibition. I was transfixed and lost all sense of time. I learned years later that he painted this just before shooting himself. Another experience was [what I call my] 'foot of the cross' experience about eight years ago.

[Note: in the passage that follows he exemplifies the apparent ease with which most mystics can enter the transcendent realm, having spontaneously "used" external stimuli and his own, made-up exercises to transcend, as well as having had previous experiences upon which to draw.]

"The 'foot of the cross' exercise is a spiritual process of sorts, in which I imaginatively place myself at the foot of the cross, and then a sense of deep humility comes to me as I realize that God is present. I don't exactly think back to specific transcendent situations—the spiritual exercises serve as that reminder. By knowing these have occurred, I can let them happen again.

"I find these extremely helpful and fruitful to me, to my development. These spiritual exercises are quite simple actually and yet are profound enough to result in a kind of dropping of barriers. I join a reality which is for me healing and—as in the 'foot of the cross' exercise—humble me.

"Now I just think of those exercises . . . and I am transported to that cluster of feelings which accompanied the original experience."

Of his ongoing spiritual study and "place" along the path, he wrote describing his thoughts and readings in typically abstract language:

"I am reading and studying C.F. Kelly on Meister Eckhart and find it helpful to my growth. A deep comparison of Saint Francis with Meister Eckhart would be splendid as they complement each other. A fusion might resemble Jesus.

"C.F. Kelly closes his Meister Eckhart commentary on divine knowledge with this quote:

" 'To my outward self all creatures are known as creatures—for instance, as wine, bread or meat. But to my inner self all individuality is not known as creatures, rather as gifts of God. To my innermost self, however, they are known not as gifts of God, but as eternally not other.'

"It was this passage to which I referred on the phone, realizing that I'm in the middle degree [i.e., of his journey along the way] and have some anticipations of what the highest degree may be like."

Case Study # 2
Housewife and Mother

This woman lives in a spacious, contemporary home overlooking the Pacific Ocean. The house sits near a cliff on an open meadow. It is orderly and neat. Apart from the sound of the ocean and the humming motor of a huge fish tank with tropical fish, the house is silent.

This study participant has been married for twenty plus years, has two children, and—with the exception of teaching a Yoga class once each week for the last eight years—her primary occupation is being a wife and mother.

Of her homemaking role and life's philosophy she said:

"What makes life meaningful to me is something beautiful to see, hear or smell every day. Something to look forward to. A sense of my being a positive force in someone else's life—for example, my husband's or child's or a friend's life. I feel I'm creative when I create a pleasant atmosphere for my family to relax and enjoy *their* lives.

"I've been married for twenty years, through good and not-so-good times, and have kept it a good relationship. I've always been here when my children needed me, and I try to set a good example with my behavior and my personal philosophy.

"I've come to the point in my life where I don't attend social gatherings unless it's really necessary. This came about by my feeling a sense of wasted time when I found myself talking about meaningless things; after a while, I noticed my mind just drifting away from these kinds of conversations. Negative, judgmental attitudes of many people were depressing to me. Now—although a large part of my day is spent planning family meals and taking care of the house—I have more time to enjoy the things I like (one of which is *not* cooking!). I stay on top of housework so that it never gets out of hand, never piles up to be a big job. I keep our debts to a minimum. I eat and exercise properly so that there is no worry about health, and I follow something disliked with something nice.

[Note: Here we see the ease with which self-discipline, doing for others and a willingness to submit to simplify life take over the personality. Her remark about feeling a sense of wasted time when with most other people was a typical one for most of the people in the study who also were quick to abandon "meaningless" activities.]

"Relatives wonder why I don't visit them when I'm in their area, and friends wonder at my difficulty in holding a train of thought when I'm around them in social situations. Once, for example, a friend confessed to me that he had to 'explain' my husband (who is also a private person) and me to his friends.

"This is fine with me. I have no need for approval from others for my thinking and way of being. I don't mind being thought of as weird. I enjoy being alone.

"If I'm ever down, if life ever lacks meaning for me, I take a long walk. I notice all the little things—microscopic flowers, insects, bark, spider webs, bird songs, water dripping, pine cones popping—I've done this ever since I was a child and it always opens me up to a wonderful feeling. I believe that if things don't turn out the way I want, it's because there's a better way up ahead. I've gotten everything I've ever wanted, and some things I only thought I wanted. So I feel very lucky in all respects, and very happy too. There's really nothing I need or want to be happy—I am fulfilled right now."

About her peak experiences and her ability to communicate these to her family:

"I experience these episodes of great happiness, a welling up of joy or ecstasy inside myself about two or three times per week—very frequently now. My husband might reject everything I say about these things, but when I see him over in the living room I think he's testing out some meditation technique, trying to get to this place in consciousness that I've been describing to him. Of course, when I ask him what he's doing, he says to me, 'I'm resting.' And, I just leave it at that.

"My son, however, has similar experiences to mine. He's quite dyslexic and I'm beginning to think that there's something about that physical state that may prompt transcending. I read that Einstein was dyslexic and told my son that, and he seemed to like having a connection with Einstein.

"Once my son had a fever—he was just a little boy then. He left his body during that fevered state: he got so scared. He was crying for me, and when I came in he was in tears, saying that he was in a corner of the room. About the same time, after he was well of course, he began to see the aura around flowers. He's very sensitive, very much like me. I'd say he's developed in this area since then, he was around seven then, and he's further along now as a result of those early experiences.

"He likes to walk as I do, and see all the little things—the tiny flowers and insects and ways of nature."

About her life-goals she added:

"Maybe I don't need to have a goal. I really don't know if I have any more goals—to have a goal means you have to pick a spot you want to reach eventually. That takes the fun out of it for me. I just try to have a little fun each day, enjoy every day for itself. I like the spot I'm in, right here and right now.

"I have a perfect life. I don't feel I have to work toward a perfect life—it's already here for me.

"As for some of the larger social movements—like Women's Lib—that doesn't touch me. I've always felt liberated. I've never had to compete in the working field because my work has been to be a wife and mother. Also, I'd like to say that I have no fear of aging whatsoever, no fear of death. I feel immortal."

Case Study # 3
Writer/Poet (Male)

This man currently lives in his own studio "space," a neatly furnished room in the home of a family of friends. He is in his thirties, and has a neat, focused appearance. The room is immaculate, somewhat sparsely furnished except for a number of books and a rather cluttered writing table full of papers and reference works. The studio overlooks a forest meadow; beyond it about two miles away is the Pacific Ocean.

This study participant is single, a college graduate who now writes poetry and also teaches self-development seminars (i.e., seminars about subjects similar to the themes of this book). He says that to his best recollection his mystic interests started developing at about the age of twenty-nine due to certain drug-induced peak experiences:

"These opened me up to nature, punctured a shield of

some sort. Thereafter aesthetics, history, the physical earth and sciences were blended for me. I felt completely related to everything. These experiences 'purified' my perception, although I felt originally to be in a sort of 'dark night' process in which I was lost. As I look back on that period it was a beginning point for me, not an ending. It was a start of that which I now call 'sympathetic magic,' in which disbelief and doubt are suspended. These experiences are what opened me up to my own inner promptings."

Of his peak experiences, he said this:

"There is a unity consciousness in these times for me—an experience which has nothing to do with time, a point of wholeness felt concretely. I can be picking lenses for a camera or doing something quite mundane, or even be in a problem-solving situation, and I'm never *not* in that space.

"I call this a 'silent space' period, an intensity that is functioning within me while I'm in activity. For example, I can be in a highly active situation, with others, and feel quiet space within me. Or I can be alone and be everything *but* quiet inside. This space within, for want of a better phrase, is also something that allows me to see that in a time of trouble I can have very positive results. It's as if I'm totally guided from within now, and thus am always perfectly directed."

[Note: in the previous comments and those that follow, we hear of the ease with which he "enters" the Transcendent realm—the same as with our other two study participants. In this man's case, however, the Absolute remains in consciousness for what seem to be long stretches of time. Also in a similar way to the second participant, there is the same non-striving attitude, although in this case it is a goal-less way of being quite active in the world. Again, with this participant we hear about the difficulty of being with others whose world-view and consciousness are not aligned to the Absolute, to wholeness.]

"It's a strange thing, but when you have this wholeness

you have everything. It's strengthening. When this energy is there, ultimately what you need isn't material. You need very little—I mean I can live with practically nothing now. The challenge that remains is other people's values and consciousness. But the bedrock within me is wholeness.''

As for intimacy, he said:

"You cannot have a true relationship without having that space developed within you—because with it you can stand alone, so now you can *choose* a relationship. Everything—even my ability to relate to others, to be truthful to them and to myself—comes from this bedrock of silence within.

"In terms of goals, I no longer think it's a question of 'my' wanting anything. The energy in me, that which I call the 'bedrock of wholeness,' dictates what happens next. If I get receptive enough to it, if I get sympathetic enough, I hear the words being shaped within me—through my being I am shaped. There is, however, a simultaneousness to this: it's not a question of me *or* It—we are one. The one becomes two and then . . . then it sort of takes on a third to make it whole. This is difficult to describe. The third element is a state, is the basis of the oneness and is inseparable from That. From this third I am open to All in All.''

[Note: in this next passage, he describes the way in which his feelings of separateness have all but disappeared, reminding us of 2 Corinthians 3:18, "We shall be completely transformed and changed into God," the goal of all true mystics. Moreover, in the previous expression this participant reflects the fully developed mystic's stance—as did the housewife and mother before him—of needing nothing because he has it all, and not only that, but in his case the understanding, the certainty that the two—the Transcendent and himself—are one. Again, in the following words about fragmentation and separation, we hear the theme of oneness.]

"Now I see that fragmentation is what separates us. There

is no separation in truth, not when one is whole inside. The meaning *is* in life, life itself is the meaning. That silence, that whole, that bedrock within—that's the meaning, energy and purpose of it all. Nothing else is needed. Epiphany, to me, is opening up to that space."

Of his own life-journey, his life-transition, he said:

"I see that in the last two or three years I've changed. I've always had a place separate from others. Even when I was in a major relationship, I've been in the world but not of it—I was always somewhat detached. It is a recent development for me that I can be with others, with large numbers of people, and when I am with them, I am still in a sea of silence. I carry that with me. As a result, I now am balancing the two—relatedness and isolation, more than I ever have before."

Of his present life and daily schedule, he added:

"I do have a discipline: it's a sort of walking meditation, Yoga meditation, in which I become mindful as I walk and during my daily, rather lengthy walks, find that I integrate my inner quietness into my activity.

[Note: this is similar, in practice, to the woman who talked about the wonderful feeling she entered when she went for a walk attending, during her walk, to all the "little things" around her. This mindfulness, as the Orientals would call it, is apparently something each enters into quite naturally, as a self-designed device to produce the Transcendent awareness in consciousness.]

"I've always been interested in the monastic life, and never had it in my head to do much else. That priority set the ground around my activities, and I suppose I had the attributes for it too. I'd say the characteristics within me set the focus for me. But lately, as I've already mentioned, I'm seeing a change toward new activities—I'm doing so many things now which I'd never even thought about before.

"In the past, I've found it an obstacle to juggle my inner

needs with the material, practical and survival issues of life. Now I see that when the right energy is there, there are very few obstacles remaining. My work is my life, is my play, is my being in the world.

"You asked what Christ means to me. I'd answer that there are certain people who appear to have a path, who follow it with intensity. He had a resonance which exemplified God. Mother Teresa has a handle like that.

"You also asked if I ever go to church. I'm never not in church."

Part Three:

The Way of Wholeness

Mention is made of two classes of yogis: hidden and the known. Those who have renounced the world are the "known" yogis: all recognize them. But the "hidden" yogis live in the world. They are not known. [Sri Ramakrishna, *The Gospel of Sri Ramakrishna*]

It is not to be learned by world-flight, running away from things, turning solitary and going apart from the world. Rather, one must learn an inner solitude, wherever or with whomsoever he may be. [*Meister Eckhart:* A Modern Translation]

9

The Look of Wholeness

> Calmness of mind does not mean you should stop your activity. Real calmness should be found in activity itself. [Ram Dass][1]

As the study participants expressed, the actualizing individual grows in self-awareness, in firm identity: he becomes guided by his interior truths, ultimately growing keenly receptive to what is, for him, real and worthwhile, as well as to what is superfluous or dishonest. It is this knowledge, and the actions which flow from it, which help him make a radical break with ordinary life—*not* the location in which he lives, his occupation, his economic or marital status, or any other mechanical aspect of his life and self-expression.

When speaking of social and self-transcendence we are talking primarily of that life-experience which is tending toward authenticity, a life ridding itself of rigid, false attitudes, culturally imposed beliefs and expectations. Be assured that such a life cannot be identified by the way it "looks" externally. No mood-making, postures of saintliness or overt actions of charity qualify us as authentic. The point of full personhood, as was pointed out in the earliest section of this book, is this: that whoever finds out what is, for him, good and holds fast to it becomes whole.

This is a significant issue in the development of the self

because the concept of finding and expressing one's good must not be equated with narcissism or hedonism. When I refer to "a person's good" I mean those traits, values and qualities which represent the source of his humanity, his individuality, his truest self. The entire process of expressing this good requires a setting of standards for one's entire life. It means knowing what is worth living for, as well as what is worth dying for. It means learning how to positively rebel against our own unconscious living as well as against those things—however innocent and warming—in society that would have us silence our unique dignity, our best self. The remarks of the study participants may lead some readers to think that a physical break with conventional life is necessary in order to become actualized. Nothing could be further from the truth.

While the study participants represent vivid examples of actualizing personalities, they do not have a corner on the market. *How* someone lives (i.e., his life-choices, where he resides, the material goods he keeps or gives away, etc.) is much less relevant to the wholeness issue than *who* the person is—what he is like—as an individual.

The objective of social and self-transcendence is to "be in the world, but not of it," to use a scriptural injunction. Detachment from the world's idea of what is good or proper is an absolute requisite in order to be one's own person. But detachment does not mean withdrawal. Nor does it mean those most common types of non-conformity people use to protest society's falsehoods: vain little adjustments of dress or diet, neurotic self-involvement and self-pity, the psychosomatic inability to function, or, worse, the psychotic, perhaps even criminal, anti-social or insane outlet which so negatively poisons everything it touches. These pathetic, futile attempts to voice frustration and stand out as a person are completely misdirected and inadequate to meet the kind of potent, positive growth process I am describing in these pages.

By detachment I mean the kind of objectivity which allows an individual to live productively within society while at the same time becoming centered in that "bedrock of wholeness"—as one study participant called the higher Self—which is his, and society's, highest good. This is requisite to knowing what *is* good, as well as to knowing when one is being swayed by, intimidated by or even angered by conventional directives. Almost no one wants to develop this kind of detachment, because it requires giving up the security of being an "adjusted" person—it requires, ultimately, that the individual *act* on behalf of what he identifies as good.

Almost everyone believes that he must adjust to society, that this adjustment is what makes for health, happiness and appropriate living among one's neighbors—even more importantly, that adjustments make for mental health. As mentioned earlier, it is the healthiest of our species who apparently take the "adjustment" matter into their own hands, deciding for themselves to what they will and will not pay homage.

As long as two decades ago, psychiatrist Robert Lindner wrote about the dangers of blind adjustment. In several works, he outlined the natural tension existing between society's need for order, structure and predictability and man's inherent drive to express what is most sacred within himself. To Lindner, the word "adjustment" was the "theme of our swan song"—the word by which we killed our own will and spirit:

> *You must adjust* . . . this is the motto inscribed on the walls of every nursery, and the process that breaks the spirit are initiated there. . . . Slowly and subtly, the infant is shaped to the prevailing pattern, his needs for love and care turned against him as weapons to enforce submission. Uniqueness, individuality, difference—these are viewed with horror, even shame, at the very least they are treated like diseases, and a regiment of specialists are available today to "cure" the child who will not or cannot conform.[2]

The independent, whole person is often perceived as a rule-breaker, as someone who stands apart. In fact, he may simply be guilty of detached, creative thinking—looking at the world, at problems, in a fresh, unconventional way. I have written extensively about the problems faced by independent thinkers in American industry[3] and need not dwell on the individual vs. society issue here. Suffice it to say that initially, the actualizing person (who dares to act on the insights and truths his own mind and feelings provide him) may appear to be a rebel. This is especially true, as we have seen, in the early stages of social-transcendence when he is pulling away from the way he has always responded to life. Eventually, in his maturity, however—particularly when personality wholeness is well established—he actually *serves* society. He has no choice but to serve it because as an actualizing personality he comes to see society—others—as himself, sees the interrelationship of the part to the whole, understands that what he is and does as a person makes up the quality and goodness of society.

And this is the irony: that the person becomes a good steward to society through the very uniqueness and individuality which society would have him thwart through the virtue of "adjustment."

In these final chapters we leave the study participants in order to review and organize what their life-statements can teach us about increasing our own uniqueness and individuality.

There are a variety of life-styles in which the men and women interviewed in these pages have obtained social and self-transcendence. Some live alone. Others structure solitary, private time into their married, occupational or recreational lives by eliminating unwanted activities and by streamlining the way in which they use time, money and their attention. Individuality—social and self-transcendence—is an ageless, genderless and cultureless issue. Anyone, of any age and any culture, having the sincerity of heart and the strength of intention to identify and express what for him is true and good, can be whole.

The study participants have, as a group, presented themselves as having three distinct skills which I am now convinced are the hallmark of health and the capacity to grow. I call these qualities *skills* because they can be learned, developed, and then used on behalf of life. Furthermore, the qualities are aptitudes because they may be—to some degree or another—natural endowments, yet anyone can tap these qualities in himself and become more whole.

First, they are *autonomous and authentic* persons. Each has at least a high enough degree of self-esteem that he is willing to act on behalf of what is, for him, real and worthwhile. Each also has the self-trust and self-reliance to know what he is about as a person, to identify—perhaps even speak up for and act out—what is valuable, what he aspires to, what is meaningful. These are persons who have the necessary energy, determination and resourcefulness to assertively opt for a life they find worth living.

It takes high self-esteem and self-trust to sacrifice collective opinion, security, customs, guarantees in favor of that which one prefers and thinks is best. To sacrifice safe and direct routes of accomplishment—maybe even accomplishment itself as it is usually defined—also requires inner strength and faith. By eliminating excessive distractions (for example, socializing—which many in the study said no longer had appeal for them—) or by scaling down their debts, possessions and obligations, the study participants demonstrate what types of sacrifices they felt compelled to make on behalf of their own growth.

The next quality the group as a whole represents is *adaptability*. None was so rigidly tied to one course of action or to one narrow belief system that he couldn't adjust to environmental pressures or changes. Those that gave up urban living for rural life-styles and who learned to live without electricity or other modern conveniences, those whose income was decreased by their self-styled lives of "voluntary simplicity," those who showed their increasing ability to rid life of its hypocrisies and morbid distortions or who said "goodbye" to toxic relationships, or who acted against something in their community they felt to be unjust, unfair—no matter how painful such goodbyes or actions were emotionally—show us why being adaptable is necessary to growth. If we cannot make it without old habits, toxic relationships, our addictions—whatever they might be—we are not free to choose our good. And while we are in the early stages of choosing that good, there is much to tolerate which calls for adaptability.

Lastly, and each of these characteristics embodies a cluster of other traits, aptitudes and skills, the study participants illustrate what it means to be *intuitive*. By becoming more capable of listening to his inner voice, each also reaps the rich rewards of the inner self: knowledge gained from the deepest self, the non-logical, non-rational self, knowledge which gives shape to life, actions and being. Whether it is gained through prayer, contemplation, study, walks in the woods or just time spent alone gazing out a window or thinking, each study participant spoke about insights, feelings and promptings from within that we can only describe as intuition. These awarenesses proved to be tremendously healing and helpful in their growth, life-choices, and in letting them know they were on the right path, even though it may have been a most difficult, stony path. More importantly than the inner guidance they receive may be the fact that each is *open to*, responsive to his own inner voice, however dimly audible, his own idea of what his life should be, what course it should take.

Factors such as whether an individual is married or single, working or retired, wealthy or poor, in business or barely making ends meet with a part-time job are immaterial to the quest for wholeness. What *is* essential however is that the individual designs his life so that he grows in awareness, gains strength to respond truthfully and ethically to everyday life, work and relational demands. His "truthful" response may be the exact opposite to what others expect and want him to do. That is precisely the point of wholeness, and the reason the adjustment issue was raised earlier: the actualizing person tends to obey his inner directive regardless of any cry of outrage or criticism from society, family, co-workers and friends.

A client of mine, one of the most integrated, whole and talented young executives I have had the privilege of working with, serves as a good example in this matter. He recently decided to leave one corporation for another against the wishes of those he respects. Circumstances were such in the first corporation that his path to a more senior position was blocked. Because he is chronologically younger than every other senior officer, he was expected to stay and patiently "wait his turn" for promotion. But his leadership drive, giftedness and sense of destiny provided fuel to his desire for a top spot in a major corporation, so he chose to leave. His colleagues and friends were shocked: they hadn't expected him to leave, since leaving was the harder course of action. He could have stayed put, earned a tremendous salary for five more years in what was (and still is) a nationally prestigious position, and then—after waiting his turn in properly "adjusted" fashion—would have been promoted to the top spot he wanted, probably before he was forty years old. Staying would have been the safer, more acceptable decision. No one expected him to take the more challenging, riskier route.

But he felt differently—felt pushed from within to leave. "This isn't even clear to me," he explained. "I don't really have a concrete picture of the message that I'm getting from within myself, but I have a sense that I'm going to have several careers." He then listed three very diverse careers in general terms and continued, "I know that people feel I should stay here and wait. But even though I might be thought to be impatient, maybe egotistical—anyone would be happy to wait, what gives me the audacity to move on?—I feel I must leave." His intuition about what he needed to do, and the fact that he was receptive to the cues and signals from inside himself, are the exact aptitudes which give his decision-making and actions such power, such good probability of succeeding.

However, this type of action—based as it is on illogical and unpopular "reasons" (i.e., unconscious stirrings and unclear, vague images) is what makes growth toward wholeness so disliked. Even though, on the surface, we see one another making self-improvement attempts, these attempts barely scratch the surface of the real self. As previous chapters have indicated, wholeness is not an easy assignment to tackle, and being whole doesn't always "look" very attractive to others. The mavericks, the aberrants, the mal-adapted (or non-conformists): these are the persons most likely to "sell all," risk everything, on behalf of their growth. Unfortunately, such individuals do not always make it all the way—they get sidetracked, may be ambivalent or weakly motivated—so the path continues to be an unattractive one.

Telling the truth about our needs, insights and convictions takes enormous courage and strength. Almost no one does it completely, and that may be the better part of wisdom. Almost no one does even a bit of this truth-telling without resistance. When one voices who he really is and wants, he runs the risk of going against everything the world (i.e., family, friends, community) holds dear, as well as confronting what he thought was important but no longer values. Often such a one is called (and calls himself) "selfish." Worst of all, perhaps most frightening of all, he comes up against his own self-doubts about what he is doing, his fears about what he might do or has done in the past, his need to conform, his desire to please others, to possess security, his wish to belong. These emotions and needs are real in one sense, and can keep an individual stuck in an untenable situation for years. Certainly such emotions can prevent him from hearing his innermost self, protecting him from having insights that would jeopardize a secure, adjusted life.

Yet it is clear that the actualized, whole personality develops *only as* the individual discovers and expresses what he really is inside. That is the cost and currency of wholeness. To do that, the person must accept himself, unconditionally. Moreover, there doesn't seem to be any guide, course of study or experience so conductive to personality as is time, reflection, inner and outer silence and solitude. In order to examine these elements and see how they promote wholeness—how they might cultivate the three major qualities of wholeness: authenticity, adaptability and intuition—I would like to first speak about two rather general abilities: patience and self-acceptance. Again, these qualities I have termed abilities because they can be learned. These add much to a person's health—both mental and physical—and not enough has been written about the value of these two qualities to wholeness.

The study participants are good guides for us here, since we see in reviewing their comments that their growing interior strength and stewardly or transcendent world-view came about gradually. In many cases we heard people describe a several year life-change. In some cases we heard comments like, "I knew it was something I had to do, even if it took the rest of my life." With the exception of those intense—and rare—conversion experiences, such as the one Saint Paul apparently underwent, it is likely that wholeness comes incrementally, over a period of many years—not in a flash of illumination or momentous, "instant" life-change. It is true that life-changing insights happen in out-of-time instances. But insights must be translated into action if they are to remedy our previous mis-perceptions, and the decisions which grew out of these, if they are to transform the quality and direction of life itself.

Time—and therefore patience—is an important, perhaps a first, requisite for self-development. Anyone whose sense of urgency or self-critical desire for immediate "perfection" is such that he wants to improve immediately is probably suffering from such low self-esteem and self-defeating expectations that he is setting himself up for failure—a failure which then further intensifies the self-loathing which set up the urgency to be perfect in the first place. Such motives are usually stimulated by our idealized version of ourselves—usually an unblemished image of ourselves that we believe will impress others, such as being superbly powerful or intelligent or beautiful, an image we *need*, much as we need to impress others, because—within ourselves—we really feel impoverished, inadequate, powerless.

These mental pictures are self-defeating to the personality which, in its deepest sense, is quite ordinary. By ordinary I don't mean commonplace. Rather I mean natural, unpretentious, or genuine, complete in what it is and what it isn't.

We cannot get to our wholeness through self-loathing, through shame, a forced or a rushed "program." Pushing and brutalizing ourselves into self-improvement projects often intensifies and reinforces the very feelings of inadequacy and incompetence we want to be rid of. Indeed, we can only get "there" when we accept ourselves where we are, here and now, when we subjectively let ourselves be. Just as a baby's teeth come in when they are ready to—and not when their parents pull them up out of the baby's gums—we had best think of our growth as something completely natural that will occur in time. As the American psychiatrist Fritz Kunkel once said, our problem is not to light the light. It is simply to remove the obstacles. Our only solution, it seems to me, is to get stronger within ourselves and not have too idealized a picture of where we wish to go, not to criticize and blame ourselves for what we are right now.

Some of the techniques I will describe in the next chapter give power and inner strength to an individual and actually increase his ability to wait, to be patient, increase his ability to tolerate his flaws.

However, these techniques demand a price. They take time. They require regular practice. Developing patience is a first skill that an individual may wish to consider in his quest for wholeness so these techniques exact the very currency the person needs to pay. As we review the study participants' comments, what we see is their willingness to take their time. One participant described his inability to rid himself of a bad habit this way: "I've discovered that if I try to force myself into changing, the habit persists. It takes on a life of its own. If I can feel that I'm all right the way I am, that I really don't have to change in order to like myself, the habit begins to leave me. So I'm giving this thing another decade or so to work its way out of my being." This patient, self-accepting attitude is not one that most people can adopt—which may be the reason so many who try to do battle against their over-indulgences (e.g., overweight, alcohol consumption, smoking, etc.) fail.

It is our own vanity that makes us think there is possibility for stainless perfection. The introvert, for example, who thinks he must be a gregarious extrovert to be perfect is rejecting what he really is in the hopes of being flawless. His best self—his blemish-free self, if there is such a being—can best come into his life by his accepting his tendency toward introversion, and not forcing some other, artificial trait upon himself. If he can accept himself as a reserved, reflective man and just let himself alone (psychically speaking) chances are good that in his more relaxed state he will begin to enjoy other people, will feel like talking freely with them, might even enjoy socializing from time to time. Wholeness is not something which arrives by our willing it, nor does it come by our executing any intellectual formula. If anything, the reverse is true. By relaxing our grip on the inordinate need for perfection we create a better emotional atmosphere to experience actualization.

We are healed to the extent that we love ourselves as we are right now—blemishes, vulnerabilities and all—not as we wish we will be at some time in some distant future. In other words, we cannot reject ourselves today and expect to accept ourselves tomorrow. Only self-acceptance, which is to say love, can bring our wholeness into being, and we gain that ability by practicing it on ourselves—and on others, if we can—now.

Of course, there is a Catch-22 inherent in this, which can only be resolved by illogical, transcendent thinking. Because we must accept ourselves as we are now, while simultaneously holding in our minds the knowledge that we want to eliminate the things in us that impede our growth, things that may be self-defeating or humiliating to us, we must transcend the dilemma, rise above it. It is self-hate which keeps each of us from our best self, self-hate which keeps in place all the limitation, hopelessness and shame that we experience. The only cure, as I've come to know it, is to love ourselves even as we do things that we know, intellectually, or that we feel, subjectively, to be unacceptable—love ourselves even as we experience our shame, self-loathing and inadequacies.

These days I often suggest to my clients that they adopt this attitude when I see them struggling with some personal flaw. The attitude is really a conceptual posture of unconditional love more than a technique. It is a mental-set, an inner stance that goes something like this: "I've not yet rid myself of this habit (or emotion, or attitude, or toxic relationship, addiction, etc.) but I'm sure—in time—I'll outgrow it, much as I outgrew other limiting habits (traits, attitudes, emotions, etc.) in childhood. I'll just be patient with myself, do everything I can which builds my self-respect, things which inspire me and others, while trusting that in the months to come this limitation will resolve itself."

If a person can truthfully embrace himself in this way— which is probably nothing more than self-forgiveness, forgiving himself for being imperfect—usually the problem or trait disappears in time. The trick is to wholeheartedly mean it. This stance is not so different than the biblical lesson in the New Testament which tells us to love the very one who is hard to love. Didn't Christ continually teach that it didn't take any special goodness to do a man a good turn who has first done one for us? "And if you salute only your brethren, what more are you doing than others?" (Mt 5:47). To love your enemies must mean that we are to love ourselves even when we are our own enemy. Yet such love, such generosity of heart, is inordinately hard to muster.

Our Western culture's emphasis on instant cure-alls and media perfection and flashy, exterior achievements makes self-acceptance almost impossible. One client, a powerfully successful entrepreneur, was also grossly overweight, and always in search of a miracle diet. When I suggested that his overeating might be a symptom of his own self-destruction, his own self-loathing, and that it might disappear if he could accept himself as worthwhile *even as* he saw himself fat, unable to control his eating, he told me that I was talking "moon language." He said that he couldn't stand to accept himself as fat. "If I accept myself as I am, I'll never change. I'll just keep on eating." To this day he is still gaining and losing and gaining weight.

There is a way out—a way to develop patience, self-acceptance and a more generous heart. Any number of solitary disciplines and practices, which our next chapter describes, are available to those who would be whole. These open the way for the intuition to develop, they set the stage for a special kind of bonding (a bonding-unto-self) which precedes actualizations, and they also give rest to a stressed and weary body. These practices provide time-out to learn about ourselves, to get stronger from within, to gain the courage and energy so that we are *able*—gaining the skills—to act on behalf of what we know to be our highest good. Most important, these practices structure into everyday life the elements of solitude, silence and self-awareness. Without physically having to change anything in conventional life we can promote the kind of perceptual detachment which has been discussed as requisite to personality health.

10

Solitude and Silence in the
Development of Wholeness

At the end of my dialogue of prayer, I've developed a
pattern:
>   In my contingency and imperfectness, I need you,
>   For your caring, I love you,
>   For your sustaining, I trust you,
>   For your holiness, I worship you,
>   My Lord and My God.
I've discovered that the closeness which I crave,
though not humanly present, is divinely right here all
the time. My aloneness may be what I need to become
dependent and open toward God directly. [Participant,
Alabama]

Throughout the ages silence has been considered a way, a discipline, by which people could refine and deepen themselves.
Most monastic orders have vows of silence whereby the individual directs all his physical and mental energies toward inner
growth and God. Some churches—the Quakers for example—
fully value silence to this day and conduct their services largely
in an atmosphere of silence.

It is in silence that our reflective ability—and our need to
reflect—is born. In silence we grow more aware: sounds, however distant, or the absence of them, bring out the hidden parts
of our personality, triggering thoughts and various fleeting

phenomena in our body and attention. In silence, we perceive the ineffable, that which cannot be verbalized, cannot be made concrete. In silence and solitude our individuality is affirmed. As we cease to speak, sitting or speaking quietly, within our own hearts and mind, we confront our past actions, aspirations, our most cherished dream figures. Not only do we meet ourselves in silence, but the silence heals us as well, for it is here, in the still, immovable changeless aspects of our very own self, that we find the safety to go through our pain, and ultimately the safety to meet our most sacred, private self, the self we are at the core of our being. Thus we rediscover and renew ourselves at the heart.

Something in us—our energy, life-source, our positive will to live—is strengthened by silence, just as our physical bodies are strengthened by sleep. It is not just the absence of sounds but the presence of a positive, complete world in itself—a world in which it is permissible, even desirable, to see ourselves, accept ourselves, as we really are. The Swiss philosopher Max Picard writes of the benefits of silence in this way:

> Where silence is, man is observed by silence. Silence looks at man more than man looks at silence. Man does not put silence to the test.[1]

Silence can be our yoga, our form of self-discipline. We will look more closely at a variety of forms of yoga in a few paragraphs, but at this point it is interesting to note that Swami Paramananda, one of the first Hindu teachers to impact the United States, taught that silence could cultivate patience in us.

> The deep things do not come suddenly. Let us be patient—with ourselves. We may recognize many defects in our natures . . . it can all be removed. Go on working silently.

Silence and patience go together. Silence has wonderful creative power. Make a study of the lives of great men. They conceive an idea but they do not go out and shout it before the world; they think silently and work quietly until they realize their ideal.[2]

While many find it near to impossible to arrange their lives in ways that mirror the study participants, almost anyone who really wants to can carve out a time and place during each day in which to be silent—to sit quietly, perhaps with eyes closed, or—as a friend of mine does—to just relegate a portion of each evening to silence, where no telephones no television or radio interrupt her time. It is in silence that she has her evening meal and in silence that she spends an entire afternoon each Sunday. She has found that these periods organize and center her life and that much energy for new ideas and projects has come about as a result of this discipline. For those who say they are too busy to add such a discipline, my sense is that they are resisting their own growth.

It can indeed be impractical to move to the woods or to leave a secure job, family or friends. And these may not be necessary at all. What is necessary—and highly practical, as we shall see—is to create a simple routine and structure in our lives so that we can meditate, reflect, sit in quiet and grow as persons.

Any number of solitary practices assist in developing wholeness. By solitary practices I mean various formal meditations such as the ancient forms of prayer common to our Judeo-Christian mystical traditions. I also mean such practices as the Zen procedure called *zazen* or classical mantra meditations which originated in India before Christ, and which now can be learned in the West through such large organizations as the Transcendental Meditation movement or smaller, more personal instruction such as is found in the Kirpal Light Satsang.

Even some physical disciplines such as Oriental martial arts (e.g., Aikido to name but one form) or long-distance running fit the type of discipline I am describing. Because meditation is such a personal matter, it is not my aim here to recommend any one activity over another—even though I know that serious students and followers of one discipline are highly critical of some procedures and strongly recommend others. What I *am* hoping to accomplish by this discussion is to encourage readers to examine the benefits of any reliable, traditional form of meditation and then—independently—investigate which specific practice might provide the most advantages for their unique, individual needs.

Although it may seem an abrupt move for us to jump from a description of the study participants' lives to that of a discussion of meditative techniques (especially in view of the fact that the study participants didn't dwell on meditation or physical disciplines) upon closer inspection it is not so abrupt.

As we have read, the participants in this study know the importance of "time out." They have all spoken of the desire to have quality time to spend as they wish. Many live alone, by choice, and of course in this way they spend a great deal of time silently. Those who are married have described their various strategies for structuring solitude, privacy and silence into their lives. Somehow, in the quiet and completely sequestered space of their inner selves they were able to identify what they needed and arrange their lives to provide that. I am suggesting that meditation, even sitting in silence, can order our own interior thinking in such a way that the answers we need to live our lives more intelligently will come. When one's whole existence is arranged simply, as is that of so many of the study participants, then fewer distractions and encumbrances are present. When there is time to pray, reflect, read, walk about in the beauty and simplicity of nature then life has a natural ebb and flow to it which is very much like a meditation. In the words of one individual, "I don't meditate per se, but then my whole life is so balanced that I'm in a contemplative state all the time." Another said, "I've become so aware of the micro/macro phenomenon all around me that my awareness is always open. When I sit at my table and look at the colors of the trees or listen to the birds, the movement of the leaves, I am transfixed. It's as if I'm keenly awake during all activity. I've done a lot of yoga in the past, and I'd say that now my entire life is a yoga of sorts—I'm *in* every act, in every moment, in a way that provides a radiant sort of energy for me."

These benefits, this same inner posture, can be achieved by setting aside a part of each day for a time of silence and solitude. Selected meditative and solitary practices help develop personality because the still-point of being, the innermost core of self, can—at first—only be reached indirectly: through dreams, through a flash of insight, through feelings or symbols, through stilling the mind. The hope behind these paragraphs is that anyone—regardless of his age, living or economic circumstances—can develop his own wholeness in an independent, private manner through some simple life-style adjustments and by the addition of a discipline.

According to psychiatrist William Glasser, a discipline must meet six requirements if it is to help people grow:

♦ It should be non-competitive and be done, for the most part, alone.
♦ It should be a practice which is not dependent on others for execution.
♦ It should be easy to do, should not require much mental effort (e.g., straining to make the mind blank turns people away from meditation despite their sound intentions).
♦ It should be a practice which is done regularly, about one hour per day (or twice a day in equal amounts of time).
♦ It should be something that the doer *believes* will improve

his mental/physical state. He must see his own improvements, without needing an "expert" or guru to tell him he's getting better—in other words, in every respect it should build self-sufficiency rather than dependence upon another.

◆ It should be something which can be done without inordinate self-criticism or comparison to someone else's progress. The individual hurts himself, and his developmental progress, when he thinks, "I'm not running as far, fast or gracefully as John," or when he cruelly ridicules himself for the form or manner in which he sees himself doing the practice.

The sum total of accumulated meditative experiences ought to be that the individual discovers his strengths and weaknesses and comes to terms with himself as a person—nonjudgmentally. We have already seen that self-acceptance and patience are necessary corollaries to positive growth, and as we proceed it may be clearer why a discipline is so helpful in developing these same qualities. A discipline is critical to any discussion of social or self-transcendence, since these two values are, in the final analysis, a coming-to-terms with the self in an honest, accepting and self-trusting way.

As one begins a discipline, it is natural to wonder if an expert, a training course or "Master" is needed. Fortunately, little formal instruction is necessary, although some believe that the initiation process is highly instrumental in obtaining productive results. Others feel there is much to be gained through the relationship with a Master. The Bible of course makes many references to the uses of meditation; ancient Eastern and classical Judeo-Christian mystical-meditative practices became tradition without extensive, or expensive, weekend seminars. Rigorous discipline, however, on the part of the meditator, and belief in the value of the practice, have always been essential.

As to why such disciplines promote growth and personality health, it is helpful to juxtapose the characteristics and functional aspects of wholeness against the impact that selected meditative practices have upon personality health.

The realized person is one who knows himself in the Socratic sense. This implies that he is truthful to himself and others, even when that truth may bring with it the severe cost of inconvenience, rejection or even physical danger. It also means that he knows himself as he is at his best: that he has recovered his relationship with his own integrity, his previously sacrificed and discarded uniqueness, his most sacred interior self which is complete and lacks nothing. This is why, in our previous chapters on the mystic type, we saw evidence, and heard it in the words of some of this book's participants, of people who wanted nothing. They felt delighted in the simplest things, as if they had everything they could possibly want. Their satiety gives us a clue to the integration which exists in the actualized personality: the individual has resolved the dichotomies of his life, solved many problems, and is living in "Being-cognition"—in the awareness of his own creative intelligence, his own highest Self. This satisfied state of affairs should not be mistaken as a why-try, humdrum lethargy, for nothing could be further from the truth.

The interpersonal and transpersonal worlds of the completed, or actualized, individual are fully assimilated and integrated. As such the person moves spontaneously from within to without—in response to his own inner Being's promptings, values and aspirations. In his moment-to-moment living, the person moves in wonderment or awe, his consciousness saturated with a richness, a surplus, a superordinate awareness.

In relationship to others, he may be highly discriminating, preferring his own company, or the company of family and a few close friends to an endless, yet superficial, stream of relationships with people he can only know slightly. On the other hand, he may be one who moves easily in social situations, enjoying everyone and anyone he comes in contact with. At the same time, along with all these qualities, he is not simply a passive or amused or blissful observer of others and of his own values and interior life.

From insights flow actions. The actualizing personality is in process of becoming more and more purposeful, more vigorous in the areas of his interests and talents. In all other areas he may be quite mundane. But in the domain of his particular inclinations or talents, he will often show passionate involvement. Be he a parent, craftsman, thinker or artist, at the very least he will be absorbed with and propelled by his own images and psyche. He *chooses*—and this is a key competency of the actualizing personality—to turn his intra-psychic world into life-activity and realistic, i.e., workable, outcomes. This translation makes the individual seem unique to others—in fact, he *is* unique. He is tapping into a special, unknown reality, a one-of-a-kind world: his own inner world and its context. From it he shapes something tangible or concrete for self-and-others on the outside. This is why Maslow used the phrase "SA creativeness." He meant that the self-actualized personality exhibited a tendency to do *anything* creatively: cooking, homemaking, teaching, building a business, speaking, etc. He contrasted this type of creativity with that which springs from special talents like artistic or poetic gifts.

The tendency to spontaneously self-express, without inordinate fear or self-strangulation, is also one of the by-products of an individual made more potent. He is more potent because now he is propelled by the added element of energy, certainty and direction which the usual person only dreams about having but is unwilling to pay the price to possess. I feel it essential to stress and repeat that there are degrees of actualization, and that what I am primarily addressing throughout this book, and more closely in this chapter, is a *process* by which a person experiences lessened fears, a changed mind, a change of heart, an alteration of energy and will in the direction of that which is healthier, more positive, more loving, responsible, independent and life-promoting. This change gradually prompts an altered life-world-self-view. It also brings about an enhanced, more committed relationship with self and others because the individual has the strength to stick with his own project and goals, the courage to be truthful, the ability to really love the other as himself. What I am talking about now is simply a healthy, completed personality: what each of us should be (and in fact longs to be) were we whole. Actualization is our most natural destination—and this is the point where I have so much trouble with the mind-set of the majority of psycholgists, psychiatrists, social workers, etc. who, instead of guiding people out of their misery, instead of waking them up to what they could be, sustain their neurotic, separated conditions by encouraging them to adjust bravely to the world. The world should, for the most part, be helped to adjust to us, since, as the Indian mystic Thakar Singn puts it, the world is made for us—we are not made for it. The psychiatric tradition still treats actualization as if it is an oddity, a rare event. Yet I believe that to be actualized is a human being's most completely natural state which, if only he had the proper guidance and information, he could easily achieve. Sadly, the usual person misses because he is so eager to adjust himself to society's conditions for "normalcy."

Were the "average" person to take time to turn inward, to develop himself in the way under examination, his behavior, choices, activities would then also become motivated *from* within. Each act and choice would have more meaning, more fluidity. Such authentic actions are the result of a conversion process which can be experienced whether or not an individual is a grocery clerk, a grade school drop out, a nuclear scientist or a "bum." This process, happily, is the great equalizer which has little to do with where and how a person lives.

Although we have continually seen in this study that the

participants pare down their life, remove many distractions from their daily life so that they can have the time and the setting to commune with themselves and with those things which matter to them, I suspect that the desire to lead a more simplified life comes *after* the self-forgetting, transcending, integrating phenomenon has begun, and as a result of it.

While no one really knows "why" some people are blessed with the tendency toward actualization while most continue to turn their back on their best selves, the key to personality health may be found in childhood. It is here where the primary relationship of self-to-self takes on its positive or negative tone.

Researcher Maya Pines' study of children whom she called "Invulnerables" holds special interest for our discussion. In her article, "Superkids,"[3] Pines explored the reasons for the superior life success of about fifteen percent of those persons who had had horrendous early life experiences. Something in these children's traumatic early lives seemed to strengthen, rather than thwart, their development.

They not only survived, they flourished into competent, capable adults. Their personal autonomy, adaptability and intuitive brightness developed while they were still very young.

As adults, they showed themselves to be independent thinkers, while retaining good interpersonal skills. Many of the fifteen percent became community leaders. As inordinately skilled adaptors, these children may offer us the clues for optimal human development.

The traits Pines described as being helpful to adult functioning were most evident in the children of schizophrenics who had to protect themselves from their parents' illness. To survive their early environments, they developed self-defenses which then served them the rest of their lives. In the midst of physical and emotional trauma, these unusual children managed to withdraw successfully into themselves, and also were able to locate at least one healthy adult figure with whom to relate. In solitude and separateness, they sorted out and ordered their chaotic world into some sensible whole, drawing from their chaos a lasting, sustaining inner strength. From their relationship with a healthy adult they learned to relate to others. In some intuitive, mysterious way which contradicts logic they managed to grow up intact, without turning their backs on themselves, without being split in half.

Their growing up involved a long, lonely struggle—against odds most other children do not survive. Their sense of being different, unique and alone may have provided them with just the foundation for independent, intuitive thinking and autonomous behavior that they needed to protect their sanity and fend for themselves.

It is precisely the lonely task of ordering their disruptive lives and coming to terms with feelings of alienation or separateness which allowed them to develop such strong feelings of self-trust, a firm sense of who they were and of what they could—and had to—do in life. I would say that this solitary sorting out process is also what adults must do if they wish to increase their own personality health.

The normal adjustment of the usual man or woman implies his or her buying into the world view—with everything that suggests—at the expense of his or her true potentialities. Most children, for example, willingly barter their own insights, feelings and aspirations for those of their parents. In the process they grow up to have bartered their own joy, freedom, ability to love. Even consulting a psychiatrist, when the individual feels he is stuck, feels he has not been living a truthful, potent life, is no guarantee of finding release. R.D. Laing writes in the Preface to the Pelican Edition of his book, *The Divided Self:*

Psychiatry could be, and some psychiatrists are, on the side of transcendence, of genuine freedom, and of true hu-

man growth. But psychiatry can so easily be a technique of
brainwashing, of inducing behavior that is adjusted. . . .
Thus I would wish to emphasize that our "normal" "adjusted" state is too often the abdication of ecstasy, the be-
trayal of our true potentialities, that many of us are only
too successful in acquiring a false self to adapt to false realities.[4]

The other ingredient necessary to personality health,
which Pines' research subjects also possessed, is the ability to
see the self as competent, able to stick with difficulty even
when—subjectively—it is natural to quit.

Although Pines' writings did not put it this way, these
children became socially transcendent in much the same way
the adults in this study have done: *they chose to step back from
their environment in order to observe it with detachment.*[5] Although
in Pines' group the detachment and withdrawal process seems
to have happened at an earlier age, in both my study and hers
detachment seems most often to have occurred because of survival needs: the individual felt, as one man expressed to me, "I
had to back out of my situation emotionally; it was a question
of life or death—*my* life or *my* death, however gradual. I knew
I simply could not continue to exist in the situation as it was."

Harvard professor Abraham Zaleznick describes an ad-
ditional host of qualities which come to those who do manage
to pull back into themselves to establish rapport with their own
self. In his article "Managers and Leaders, Are They Different?"[6] he gives a description of leaders which sounds very
much like Pines' superkids saying that they have lives marked
by a sense of being different, of continual struggle to sort out
and make the world in which they live comprehensible.

From their earliest days, born leaders question things.
They are often alienated persons who experience a "profound
separateness," and who sort out life's questions alone. They

also face, rather than avoid, their difficulties, just as study participants spoke of facing their abysses or conflicts alone. These qualities reward Zalezniks' leader-personalities with their tough bite on life. I suggest that these traits are also essential to the actualizing personality.

Although Zaleznik and Pines were talking about leaders and unusually competent children respectively, the characteristics of these two groups *are* the characteristics of healthy well integrated people. As with those in Pines' and Zaleznik's studies, the healthy adult initiates his own development through a reflective, contemplative process. This may be very painful at the start, but later benefits the person and eventually benefits others. The individual ultimately relates to himself-and-others as a whole personality whereas previously he related as a scattered, separate one.

Self-reliance and subjective fortitude are also benefits of this reflective, contemplative procedure. At the core of the individual's inward feelings of strength are self-trust and self-respect. Having no one else to lean on, choosing not to lean on anyone else, the individual begins to lean on himself. Thus he builds a bond of trust with his own self.

Author Joseph Chilton Pearce tells us that the mind develops bonds (which he defines as forms of rapport and communication) with a primary matrix while in infancy. The primary matrix, as we might guess, is the mother.

Matrix, according to Pearce, comes from the Latin word for womb. From this word come the words 'matter,' 'material,' 'mother' and so on. Out of these conceptual frames the physical forms of life are derived. Eventually, the individual's mind shifts its mother-as-matrix feelings to the world.

When a child feels safe in his primary matrix (i.e., safe within the subjective/actual experience of his mother), he eventually believes that the world—as it forms its new matrix to the larger environment—is a safe place too.

I agree with Pearce that few children form the kind of bond that children were meant to have. In the case of Pines' group called "invulnerables" *these children learned to fend for themselves so well because they actually recreated their matrix for themselves—in a way they were their own mothers*[7]—ultimately learning to trust the new one, which, of course, was a bond-to-self. The new matrix, was one which was, for them, safe and it led to their feeling that they were safe in the world. Because they related so successfully from within to without, because as children they discovered that they could capably handle the world of others as well as circumstances, their adult life was one of enhanced competency.

Most people do not undertake this difficult personal homework of building inner strength, as previous chapters have noted. The usual man lives separated from his highest self, lives a contracted, emotionally weak life. Thus a distrusting core of feelings about self-and-matrix follow him into adult life. When someone distrusts himself, when he feels that there are a host of unpredictable circumstances to face and that other people are unknowable, or threatening, then he distrusts the world. He feels ill-prepared to strike out on his own. Strictly speaking, the average person is closed off and guarded against himself—cut off from his most capable, tender or creative self. Were he to know this self he would have to have tapped his own inner depths, would have had to be open to his own primary thought processes and inward directives.

We have seen that rich rewards come to those who reframe, reinterpret and recreate their own self-and-other paradigm. When the necessary work of bonding to self (and now I am referring to the highest self: the one mystics and theologians label "Self") has been completed, the regeneration of a new, trustworthy and even friendly matrix takes place. The individual feels subjectively safe. He is emotionally connected and experiences no separation, no splitting or fragmentation.

He doesn't *feel* isolated, separate or alone because—in a real way—he is connected, bonded, safe, "at-one-with," at home. The Indian guru, Maharishi Mahesh Yogi, calls this feeling "mother is at home." Any and every emotionally healthy, whole person has this subjective sense and is an integrator— able to fuse the opposites of his personality (and resolve outer splits and seeming contradictions) into a unified whole. He is able to do this because he has done it within himself.

This interior work of establishing self-trust, meaning and order provides those character traits (or aptitudes, as I've called these earlier) which we ultimately link with actualization. This has a chicken-or-egg quality to it: do people who face their necessary inner homework of ordering personal conflict and chaos have an inclination toward solitary, silent introspection? Or are their early lives indeed so difficult that eventually—whether in childhood or adulthood—they must think through their problems independently or disintegrate as personalities?

I'm reminded of the study participant who said that for him separation was "insanity." Apparently, the world-as-matrix for him was so dangerous and chaotic that he had to sort things out or suffer dire consequences. This suggests that there are degrees to separation: for one it means insanity, for another mild anxiety, and, for still another, just a "normal" life he has become accustomed to with some constant degree of tension or disappointment.

Whatever the degree, and whatever the cause for initially pulling away, entering the inward path, this long, solitary ordering process when effectively done is a *building* process, a positive, bonding-to-self activity. This culminates, when it is done fully, in the individual's establishing a secure foundation for thinking and acting for themselves. This means he becomes heavily, if not totally, self-referring. Also, by trusting himself for his actions and directions, he comes to be someone whom others also can trust. Of these persons, we feel they are predictable, all of a piece, understandable, knowable. Of these persons, we sense that they provide us with constant, consistent messages—rather than mixed signals or contradictions.

From both a professional and a personal standpoint, I have come to believe that adults can build a secure framework out of which to live their lives if—and it is a big if—they are willing to face the necessary work of inner regeneration: the pulling away, self-scrutiny and self-acceptance/self-trust steps which I've outlined. These all involve questioning many previously made life-decisions: how they have "adjusted" to the world, what attitudes have been formed with which they face everyday life situations, the relationships entered into (or separated from), his life's work, the attitudes with which everyday tasks are faced, and so on. The person who fears his own thoughts, who needs others too much, who is overly self-critical or severely attached to his own cultural belief systems and values may not be able to do this work.

The assignments include changing our minds about almost everything. Because we must establish a bond with ourselves—with an invisible, yet real part of ourselves—it may mean questioning the way in which we've learned to accept the world. If we view the world as unfriendly, for example, yet see that not everyone sees it in this way, this might be a good place to start. If we feel that certain things in life—say, happiness or love or doing work we enjoy—were meant for others but not for us, then that might be an area to probe: Why might we be left out of those life benefits? Where did we get our rules? Who gave us our values and expectations—where did these come from? How happy were the people who told us the world was one way or another? How fulfilled were our teachers? How much love did they express and experience?

If we are willing to face the assignment, we will have to question many previously made life-decisions and beliefs. Taking this assignment to heart offers enormous benefits: a subjective sense of safety and confidence comes to the one who finds his real self, who meets and is friendly with his own feelings, inclinations and values. He will waste little time surveying others for their opinions, or defending himself against himself (i.e., against his own desires, aspirations and feelings) and thus the ability to focus on meaningful work or relationships or on personal goals will be available to him. More of the individual is available for utilization, for enjoyment, for spontaneous relationship and expression, for playing, for living as he truly desires to live.

Yet there is an ironic twist here: the individual must establish a bond with an unknown, invisible part of himself before he can become whole. This means that he must be willing to face what heretofore he was afraid of facing—his own shadowy, perhaps demonic self, his cowardly, loathed secret self which he himself has rejected and hidden, often successfully, from others. Thus there is ample resistance and natural reluctance to start this work—a resistance almost everyone shares.

Most deny themselves the opportunity of knowing and drawing out something more in themselves. Out of fear, lethargy (usually a resistance in disguise) or indecision, they believe that such work is foolish, that people stay as they are, that change is impossible—at least for them. The whole person, on the other hand, is someone who stimulates and energizes us— even if only in our imaginations—*because* he has been strengthened from within in just this way—the way we may be avoiding.

In my professional practice, when I sense that an individual yearns for wholeness and is willing to do the requisite personal work (which, by the way, rarely involves much of my help) I usually recommend that he start meditating or at minimum take up a physical discipline which fits the conditions I specified earlier. I encourage him to take full responsibility for researching the particular discipline he wants to start as well as the responsibility for beginning.

Meditation regenerates and reconstructs the personality. In some ways it is similar to the psychotherapeutic process in that it introduces the meditator to a part of himself which he may have been avoiding. At the very least, a regular meditation program will alleviate certain physical stresses, enabling the person to feel more gratified, safer, less anxious, less despairing. In its ultimate form (and no doubt, since there are various types and schools of meditation, we have to select wisely in order to gain the ultimate benefit) and highest benefit, a meditation procedure can enable us to reap the fruits of full personhood, whether we call this enlightenment, actualization, Being, or Selfhood.

When, through an effective meditation procedure, we are introduced to parts of ourselves we may have been avoiding, we find a key to the authentic intuitive self. Perhaps we learn to gradually accept that in ourself which we have previously rejected, which has made us seem different from others. Perhaps we begin to accept, then express, that which we formerly denied. All classical forms of meditation, whether they be Western forms of prayer or chanting, or more esoteric Eastern disciplines, bring up into the awareness previously unconscious bits of past experience, eventually allowing us to assimilate these into a unified whole, or *gestalt*.

Jung wrote that the hidden self was like a shadow, and that without the shadow a person was only half himself. Many decades later, Fritz Perls, father of *gestalt* psychology, reinforced this notion by stressing the importance of *assimilation* to personality development.

By assimilation, Perls meant the taking in and absorption (through active and conscious awareness) of bits of repressed memories and past experiences which—in their unassimilated state—fragment, drain and weaken personality health. He likened the assimilation process to chewing up food, saying that undigested morsels would return, unpleasantly to cause trouble for the individual. To him, unacknowledged emotions and experiences sap energy and sow the seeds for conflict and neurosis. Of this he wrote:

> The awareness of, and the ability to endure, unwanted emotions are the *conditio sine qua non* for a successful . . . cure. This process (i.e., assimilation) forms the *via regia* to health.[8]

Meditation offers an opportunity to become aware of, endure and ultimately assimilate unwanted emotions so that they fade into the background becoming understandable in the context of our whole life and becoming endurable in that—through our meditative experience—we see ourselves, feel ourselves, watch ourselves enduring the sight and memory of these conditions.

One of the reasons that hypnosis and other types of suggestion or trance-like processes may not work in this same way is because the individual strives to attain something (even if only a relaxed state of mind), and in his striving, in this "doing," he directs his attention rather than dwelling on something simple. In meditation he becomes consciously aware of everything that passes through the mind; thus our attention "watches" the mind impartially as a by-product of the act of dwelling. This is difficult to describe to the non-meditator who has not had the experience of pure awareness which comes with meditation.

All meditation involves a dwelling upon something: a word, a flame, a mantra, a phrase, a breath. It is while the mind is occupied in this way that the attention is brought to deeper and more subtle levels of itself—eventually transcending mind so that it becomes pure awareness. The meditator develops an inner posture which (like a spotlight on his own attention) shines itself on an ever-larger scenario of thoughts and images—both in and out of meditation. While meditating, the meditator gains a front-row seat as witness to his own mental phenomenon, thus gaining objectivity over thoughts and fleeting images, since anything that can be observed objectively can be controlled.

Rather than remaining an involved actor, or a trapped experiencer, to his own emotions the meditator gradually is liberated, able to endure emotionally what, in ordinary consciousness, he felt was unendurable. What he previously avoided, suppressed or buried is brought up to his awareness. The meditator goes through an inner struggle (albeit more comfortably in most cases) much like Pines' superkids or Zaleznik's developing leaders or our study participants in their earliest stages of emotional growth. He—like all these others—now also faces, sorts out and organizes personal conflicts, resistances and inner bits of experience into an assimilated whole, all the while developing personality strength and self-trust.

Observing whatever it is that we have previously suppressed has enormous value since shying away from negative emotions only serves to drain our creative potential and energy. Repressing and pretending things are not what they are only weakens our entire character. However, more than simply allowing us to face unpleasantries objectively, when we meditate the discipline develops the personality in yet another significant way.

These solitary disciplines cultivate an inner quality—what Dr. Claude Naranjo and Professor Robert Ornstein call a "modality of being." They write:

> This presence or mode of being transforms whatever it touches . . . it might be said that the attitude or inner posture of the meditator is both his path and his goal. For the

subtle, invisible how is not merely a how to meditate, but a how to be. . . .

The practice of meditation can be better understood as a . . . persistent effort to detect and become free from all conditioning, compulsive functioning of mind and body, habitual emotional responses that may contaminate the utterly simple situation required by the participant.[9]

This procedure is capable of providing personality health. It creates in the individual a simple silent inner witness and an ethical, accepting inner stance. I said earlier that it is not necessary to withdraw physically from society or actually change a life style in order to grow whole. Social and self-transcendence are available to anyone who is seriously willing to undertake the easy self-discipline of a daily meditation period. Thus the individual can structure into his life a silence, a keener self-awareness and an obedience (i.e., to the higher self). In this way he can cultivate an inner transformation of the sort and quality I have been describing throughout this book.

There are so many forms of meditation that it would be impossible to list them all in a comparative manner here. Many solitary *physical* disciplines are more appealing to some personality types. These can be a healthy addition to overall physical and mental conditioning. Prayer, working in a journal, outside spiritual readings, some types of devotional visualization, and mindful walking can all open the attention to the never-ending action and antics of the very restless mind. However, in my opinion, only a few forms of rigorous meditation serve the conversion process which is under examination. In these practices the individual enters very deeply into his own inner silence, which promotes a level of consciousness—transcendent consciousness—not available to man in his ordinary waking state. Through this, the inner presence, the center of our real self, is made known to us—we join it, as it and the bonding-unto-self can take place.

Those who are mystically inclined are usually very naturally drawn to such practices. These persons can begin to develop intimate fellowship with that in them which is highest and most sacred. The value of meditation upon the mystic sense is described fully in the book, *Finding Grace at the Center*. In it the authors describe a traditional Christian prayer called the centering prayer and relate it to other, classical forms of meditation:

> By turning off the ordinary flow of thoughts, which reinforces one's habitual way of looking at the world, one's world begins to change . . . if you turn off your ordinary thought patterns, you enter into a new world of reality. To do this systematically, take up a position that will enable you to sit still. Close your eyes. . . . Then slow down the normal flow of thoughts by thinking just one thought. Choose a sacred word of one or two syllables that you feel comfortable with. A one-syllable word such as God or Love is best.[10]

The text continues with these simple instructions, advising the reader that, as he continues, he will enter a deeper level of reality. This reality marks a beginning, not an end-point, of development, and it is this inner reality which is the healer—not anything or anyone in the outer world. The entire prayer is to be undertaken with the presupposition of dedication to God. This path, or any way of devotion, such as is described above has great power to "open" the heart—allowing the most tender emotions and values of the spirit to emerge.

As an actualizing person attains wholeness, as he establishes a steady, constant bond with his inner self, he also establishes emotional security. This may amount to a Taoistic "let be," or—in the Judeo–Christian way of thinking—a

"God's will be done." This is not so much a futile helplessness of outer conditions as it is a faithful knowing that things will work out, will resolve, that non-resistance is the key to solving all things, for such non-resistance, and faithful acceptance is an active choice born of love.

Prayer, meditation and contemplation do more than just calm the mind or open the heart. These also steady the body. Many physicians now prescribe meditation and/or regular, non-competitive exercise (like brisk walking, yoga, jogging or swimming) for patients suffering from hypertension, over-reactive nervous systems or digestive problems. Even hyperactivity in children is now being treated with meditation rather than drugs—although perhaps not as frequently as it should be. There is no neat mind/body split. What helps the mind gain rest from its constant seeking, grasping, worrying, must also help the body. Many researchers have documented the physiological benefits of meditation.

Dr. William Glasser's study of long-term runners and meditators demonstrated that the physical benefits are woven in with psychological ones. His research indicates that a mix of blessings comes to those who are, in his words, "positively addicted" to their disciplines. Over time, these people developed:

◆ subjective feelings of inner confidence, self-trust, outward serenity, calm or grace;

◆ creative thinking aptitudes;

◆ the ability to resolve inner conflicts and/or expanded ability to spot new or varied options in problem solving;

◆ a firm sense of self, including the willingness to speak up and take action on behalf of what they sense was right and true for them;

◆ an increased ability to cope with pressure, manage stress and deal with ambiguity and change.

We can quickly see by reviewing the earlier traits listed of the actualized personality that these traits and aptitudes are one and the same.

Almost any practice will help, provided it fits the criteria listed. I am personally loathe to any organized meditation programs, with the possible exceptions of the Zen Buddhist movement, the TM program and the less well known but seemingly spotless teaching of Thakar Singh (Kirpal Light Satsang). These procedures, although very different, instruct the individual in their classic forms of meditation and then the individual is free to do the program on his own, without the trappings of organized *ashrams*, dogma or socio-political nuances. There must be many other procedures and teachings which I have not listed which do not require an individual to abandon his own religious heritage but actually strengthen him in whatever heritage he may have had. I am loathe to recommend any program which entices an individual to adopt its way of life as a condition of doing the meditation, since such enticements strike me as being the very essence of enculturation which actualization would seek to avoid and is seeking to overcome in the very first place.

There is a story that Ram Dass tells which appeals to me in this regard. It seems that God and Satan were walking along the street together when God bent down and picked something up. Curious, as always, Satan inquired of the Lord, "What is that you have there?" As the Lord gazed at the thing, glowing brightly in his hand, he replied, "This is Truth." Whereupon Satan reached out for it, saying as he grasped at it, "Here, let me have it. I'll organize it for you."

The individual who would be whole must learn to think for himself, must grow to be self-referring rather than other-world referring, must progressively design his life and his actions from his intra-psyche rather than from the rules, idols and status symbols of the outer world. Simply substituting one cultural overlay of expectations and beliefs for another one will not do. Nothing short of full authenticity will do, which, as we have seen, involves a steadfast loyalty to the demands of what we are within. As difficult as this seems to be in all its dimensions, perhaps nothing is more of a struggle than the task of accepting ourselves for what we are—warts and all, as the saying goes. Even well developed personalities, even the healthiest of individuals, have areas within themselves which they would change if they could. This too must be given up, if we wish to be healed and make ourselves whole. The author Andre Gide once said that what seems different in each of us is the rare thing we each possess. It is the one thing that gives us our worth, and that's just what we try to suppress; and we claim to love life.

For this self-acceptance work perhaps nothing, except meditation and prayer, surpasses the spiritual diary. For many years I had been recommending (and have used) a sort of journal procedure in which the individual tracks his inner growth, dreams, ideas and establishes a dialogue with himself on a regular and systematic basis. Recently, through the writings of Kirpal Singh, I have been introduced to the idea of a spiritual diary whose benefits are vast. For one thing, the individual can track his daily life from the vantage point of his own unique qualities. For spiritual followers, the diary is also a way of remembering God. Next, the diary serves as a way for the individual to confess his failings; even if he is the only one who will read his comments, at least he remains honest with himself. Kirpal Singh writes:

> Let your confessions be honestly and openly recorded in
> the various columns, so that you know where you stand

and can take rectifying action. The best and easiest way to cure your ills is to yearn to be free of them. . . . Once you become aware of a failure, you should be able to trace it to a certain situation, and this situation will help you to identify the cause of the weakness in you that has to be strengthened. By and by, the very cause of the failure will drop off by itself.[11]

The first sign that we are accepting ourselves as we are is our willingness to *look* at ourselves honestly—thus my inclination to recommend contemplative exercises and journal or diary keeping. The next step is having the humility to acknowledge that we are not perfect, that the world need not circle around us or bow to us as demi-gods in order for us to be happy. Only the brutality of our small self, egocentric self, demands flawless perfection which it interprets as that unnatural, artificial sameness which is the world's idea of perfect. Perfect can also mean complete, lacking or needing nothing, having in itself all that it needs to have. This is what I believe Christ was speaking about when he said, "You, therefore, must be perfect, as your heavenly Father is perfect" (Mt 5:48).

If we want this type of perfection—namely completion as a personality—then we must also give ourselves the time in which to grow, for this will not happen overnight. Insights come in a flash, in a burst of out-of-time experience. However it takes time to turn our insights into behaviors. In order to turn our insights and awarenesses into a new life, in order to embody what we come to know as true, we may need to organize our life so as to have the chance to grow in our daily choices and habit patterns. We will need to design our lives so that there is quiet, reflective time to become what we know we already are at some deep level. For this, we need more than our weekends, more than just a Sunday retreat. We may need to devote our whole life to this process, because in reality there is no end-point to growth.

So this is the next commitment: to discipline ourselves enough so that we will have the time we need. Saying no to endless social distractions or evenings spent in front of the television and saying no to family and friends who would have us spend our time in other meaningless ways may be ways to carve out enough time for this most essential work. Sometimes a counselor is needed for just this aspect of the work, since strong resentments may crop up when one family member (say, for example, a spouse) wishes to pursue meditation or journal keeping and another wishes life would continue as it always has.

Seeking out some help along the way may—or may not—be requisite to whatever it is we are to do: it all depends upon where we are, what the circumstance is and how we choose to see the situation. Also, our needs at one point in our growth will not be those of another point, so our helpers may change. One wise counselor told me many years ago that growth was a lifelong process so that the helpers and teachers we need for this process are sure to change. "Don't be too proud to seek assistance—this is the only practical thing to do," he told me. "And don't be too reluctant to let go when the time comes. You may need to go on for a while by yourself, and then another teacher will appear. They are all useful if you assume total responsibility for choosing them, for working with them, and for letting go when it is time."

Fritz Kunkel suggested that it is also helpful to examine the biographies of people who have lived "well-lived" lives in order to see how they overcame problems and elevated themselves during their lives. He stressed that it was not necessary to read about famous people, because within the lives of people unknown to fame we could find many illustrations of creative ways of dealing with life's obstacles and opportunities for growth.

Above all our growth must not be sought through some

harsh or artificial use of gimmicky techniques which we adopt, hoping to hype our way into wholeness. Neither does authenticity come to those whose self-talk is negative, shame or guilt producing, or who subject themselves to endless harangues about what they "should" be doing, thinking, feeling.

We have seen that it does not take inordinate material wealth or superhuman will power to live creatively. All that is needed is that each design his life to express primarily those values which are most meaningful and elegant, most life-sustaining. And we need not always look to others for help, role-models or reassurance. After a certain point it is necessary to let go of all outside help and focus in on our own strength and resourcefulness.

What we seek, seeks us. The goal of our life—whatever we want to call it—is within us, always present as the very life-source in us. All we need to do is recognize, perhaps at first through faith, that inside is a profound, mysterious power which pervades our existence and which can heal, guide and inspire us. The design or redesign of our way of life is a secondary act—and that is why there are as many ways to design life as there are people. The primary activity is to understand what is for us most authentic, most real. If, on the other hand, we try to adjust ourselves too closely, mechanistically, to that which some expert, guru or trend tells us is right and good or even required, we exchange a fuller experience of life for something less than we are worthy of.

Anyone willing to undertake the regenerative work of getting in touch with himself can experience social and self-transcendence. And these values absolutely are the natural well-springs out of which all clarifying thinking, motives and acting come. For these are the values that put us in touch with ourselves as we truly are, instead of as we may sometimes feel: limited, dark, ever-empty, superior or helpless. The inner journey, whatever its costs, and whatever form it may take, is necessary for anybody who wishes to embody in thought, word and action all that he truly loves. In this way, he comes to know and to be his ideally balanced, most wholesome and generous self: his highest Self.

Notes

Introduction

1. Marsha Sinetar, "Management in the New Age," *Personnel Journal* (September 1980): 749–55.

1. Advancement to Wholeness

1. Dorothy B. Phillips, ed., *The Choice Is Always Ours* (Illinois: Theosophical Publishing House, 1975), p. 45.
2. Paul Tillich, *The Courage To Be* (New Haven: Yale University Press, 1952), p. 28.
3. Phillips, p. 38.
4. Robert Bolt, *A Man for All Seasons* (New York: Scholastic Book Services, 1960), p. ix.
5. *Ibid.*, pp. 94–95.
6. Abraham Maslow, *Toward a Psychology of Being* (New York: The Viking Press, 1971), p. 154.
7. Clark Moustakas, *The Authentic Teacher* (Cambridge: Howard A. Doyle Printing, 1966), p. 2.

2. The First Step

1. Thomas Merton, *Contemplation in a World of Action* (New York: Image Books, 1973), pp. 124–25.

3. Practical Considerations

1. Edmund Colledge and Bernard McGinn, translators, *Meister Eckhart: The Essential Sermons, Commentaries, Treatises and Defense* (New York: Paulist Press, 1981), pp. 257–58.
2. Thomas Merton, *The Monastic Journey* (New York: Image Books, 1978), p. 106.

4. The Developmental Side of the Stewardship Pattern

1. Thomas Merton, *Thoughts in Solitude* (New York: Farrar, Straus and Giroux, 1981), p. 13.
2. For examples of early stewardship and social responsibility messages, see Ez 16:49–50, Ex 7–8, and Jer 5–26.

5. Gifts of Self as Stewardship

1. Abraham Maslow, *The Farther Reaches of Human Nature* (New York: The Viking Press, 1971), p. 301.
2. Erich Fromm, *The Art of Loving* (New York: Harper & Row, 1962), pp. 22–23.
3. Thomas Merton, *The Secular Journal* (New York: Farrar, Straus and Giroux, 1977), p. 259.
4. Colledge and McGinn, p. 189.

6. The Mystic Type Along the Way

1. Evelyn Underhill, *Mysticism* (New York: E.P. Dutton, 1961), p. 91.
2. During the editing of my manuscript, one of my friends suggested I mention that it is possible to be a mystic and live a conventional, urban-type life. Indeed this is so. A friend of mine, for example, living in southern California where her husband was re-

quired to remain for his aerospace job, is a perfect case in point. She has arranged her life so that each morning is devoted to quiet, meditative blocks of time. Many weekends of the year she manages to spend time at a rural retreat, where, along with others, she experiences the silence and solitude her spirit seems to require. In this study, however, all those who fit the mystic profile lived in solitary, rural locations, having pulled away not only emotionally from conventional life but physically too. My guess is that those with the true mystic intent who find they must live in the city or suburbs would design a life-style which would insure their privacy.

3. Underhill, p. 262.

4. Phillips, p. 155.

5. Underhill, p. 86.

6. E. Allison Peers, trans. and ed., *Dark Night of the Soul* (New York: Image Books, 1959), pp. 81–84.

7. Meher Baba, *Life at Its Best* (New York: Harper & Row, 1957), p. 51.

8. Swami Paramananda, *Christ and Oriental Ideals* (Massachusetts: The Vedanta Center, 1968), p. 119.

9. John Clarke, trans., *St. Thérèse of Lisieux: Her Last Conversations* (Washington, D.C.: ICS Publications, 1977), p. 60.

10. Franz Hartman, *The Life and Doctrines of Jacob Boehme* (New York: Macoy Publishing Co., 1929), pp. 60–61.

11. Lee Sannella, *Kundalini* (California: H.S. Dakin Co., 1978), pp. 2–4.

12. Brother Lawrence, *The Practice of the Presence of God* (New Jersey: Spire Books, 1980), p. 37.

13. Richard Maurice Bucke, *Cosmic Consciousness* (New York: E.P. Dutton and Co., Inc., 1969), p. 78.

14. Underhill, p. 87.

15. *Ibid.*

16. Colledge and McGinn, pp. 199–201.

17. Shunryu Suzuki, *Zen Mind, Beginner's Mind* (New York: Weatherhill, 1975), p. 107.

18. *Ibid.*

7. Illumination and Darkness Along the Mystic's Way

1. Maslow, p. 99.
2. *Ibid.*, p. 101.
3. Bucke, p. 225.
4. Phillips, p. 81.
5. Abraham Maslow, *Religions, Values and Peak Experiences* (England: Penguin Books, Ltd., 1970), p. 27.
6. See Phil 1:9–10; Eph 1:17–19; 3:14–19.
7. Thomas Keating, Basil Pennington, and Thomas E. Clarke, *Finding Grace at the Center* (Massachusetts: St. Bede Publications, 1979), p. 45.
8. Thomas Merton, *Contemplation in a World of Action* (New York: Image Books, 1973), p. 220.
9. *Ibid.*, p. 225.
10. Sannella, p. 64.

9. The Look of Wholeness

1. Ram Dass, *Journey of Awakening* (New York: Bantam Book, 1978), p. 138.
2. Robert Lindner, *Must You Conform?* (New York: Grove Press, Inc., 1956), p. 169.
3. Marsha Sinetar, "Entrepreneurs, Chaos and Creativity," *Sloan's Management Review*, Vol. 26, No. 2, (Winter 1985): 57–62.

10. Solitude and Silence in the Development of Wholeness

1. Max Picard, *World of Silence* (Indiana: Regency/Gateway, Inc., 1953), p. 17.
2. Swami Paramananda, *Silence as Yoga* (Massachusetts: The Vedanta Centre, 1974), pp. 22–23.
3. Maya Pines, "Superkids," *Psychology Today* (January 1979).

4. R.D. Laing, *The Divided Self* (London: Penguin Books, Ltd., 1965), Preface.

5. Pines, *art. cit.*

6. Abraham Zaleznick, "Managers and Leaders, Are They Different?" *Harvard Business Review* Vol. 55, No. 3 (May/June 1977): 67–78.

7. Pines, *art. cit.*

8. Fritz Perls, *Ego, Hunger and Aggression* (New York: Vintage Books, 1969), p. 179.

9. Claude Naranjo and Robert E. Ornstein, *On the Psychology of Meditation* (London: Penguin Books, 1971), pp. 8–9.

10. Keating, p. 12.

11. Kirpal Singh, *How To Develop Receptivity* (New Hampshire: The Sant Bani Press, 1973), pp. 11–12.

References

Benjamin, Anna S. and Hackstaff, L.H., translators. *On Free Choice of the Will*. Bobbs-Merrill Educational Publishing, 1980.

Benson, Herbert. *The Relaxation Response*. Avon Books, 1976.

Bonhoeffer, Dietrich. *The Cost of Discipleship*. Macmillan, 1963.

Campbell, Anthony. *Seven States of Consciousness*. Harper & Row, 1974.

Dass, Ram. *Journey of Awakening: A Mediator's Guidebook*. Bantam, 1978.

————. *Only Dance There Is*. Doubleday, 1974.

Delaney, Gail. *Living Your Dreams*. Harper & Row, 1981.

Glaser, William. *Positive Addiction*. Harper & Row, 1976.

Goldberg, Philip. *The Intuitive Edge*. J.P. Tarcher, 1985.

Higgins, John B. *Thomas Merton on Prayer*. Image Books, 1978.

Howes, Elizabeth B. and Moon, Sheila. *The Choice Maker*. Theosophical Publishing House, 1977.

Jones, Rufus M. *The Faith and Practice of the Quakers*. Philadelphia Yearly Meeting of the Religious Society of Friends, 1958.

Kierkegaard, Soren. *Purity of Heart*. Harper & Row, 1956.

Kunkel, Fritz. *Creation Continues*. Word Books, 1973.

Maharishi Mahesh Yogi. *Transcendental Meditation*. Allied Publishers, 1963.

Merton, Thomas. *The Way of Chuang Tzu*. New Directions, 1969.

Overstreet, H.A. *The Mature Mind*. W.W. Norton and Co., Inc., 1984.

Pearce, Joseph Chilton. *The Crack in the Cosmic Egg*. Pocket Books, 1973.

Progoff, Ira. *At a Journal Workshop: The Basic Text & Guide for Using the Intensive Journal Process*. Dialogue House, 1977.

Saint Teresa of Avila. *The Interior Castle*. Image Books, 1961.

Shorr, Joseph E. *Go See the Movie in Your Head*. Popular Library, 1977.

Thompson, T.K. *Stewardship in Contemporary Life*. New York: Association Press, 1965.

_____ . *Stewardship in Contemporary Theology*. New York: Association Press, 1960.

Wickes, Frances G. *The Inner World of Choice*. Harper & Row, 1976.

Wojtyla, Karol (Pope John Paul II). *Love and Responsibility*. Farrar, Straus and Giroux, 1982.

About the Author

Marsha Sinetar is an educator, organizational psychologist and mediator. She heads Sinetar and Associates, Inc., a human resource development firm based in Santa Rosa, California. The firm is an advisory, planning and clarification arm to large corporations undergoing wide-scale, rapid change.

Marsha has an extensive background in public sector management, as well as progressively complex leadership assignments in the private sector. She has had over a dozen articles in journals such as *The Executive, Computer Decisions, Computerworld, Personnel Journal*, and *Sloan's Management Review*. Her research and writings have progressively focused on the characteristics, thinking, and work styles of gifted leaders, creative entrepreneurs, and the whole, self-actualized person.

ORDINARY PEOPLE AS MONKS AND MYSTICS is Marsha's first book.